unlearning god

how a preacher boy
questioned the bible,
failed the code
of conduct,
wagered with god,
and found healing
from spiritual
head injuries.

- a memoir by r. leo olson

ISBN SOFTCOVER 978-0-9838106-2-9
ISBN 10: 0983810621

Edited by Zechariah Allen

For information and to see other books by R. Leo Olson, visit www.rleoolson.com.

unlearning god

r. leo olson

Dedicated to the
spiritually wounded.
Let not your
heart be troubled,
the Hound of heaven
still hunts for you.

r. leo olson

CONTENTS

r. leo olson

AUTHOR'S NOTE

Like most memoirs, the events follow a 'loose chronology' as themes developed in my life. I have left out some details, compiled conversations and changed the names of many because I didn't want to embarrass or embitter anybody. It is filled with some comedic rage, raw honesty, and some minor details have likely been misremembered.

I'm sure some will *wrongly* accuse me of hating Baptists, the Bible, and even God. I've talked myself out of writing this book many times. However, I've also been convinced by many divine promptings to write it, season it with as much love as I can muster, but write it true. Authenticity seems to be the prevailing virtue of our time. So, with apologies, here it goes.

r. leo olson

SON OF A VET

I was a good boy. I grew up on Green Lake in west Michigan. My early childhood consisted of swimming to sand bars we called sunken islands, fishing for the fish monsters of local folk lore, boating, holding-your-breath underwater contests, being a pirate and every other fun, adventurous, imaginative thing a lake has to offer a young boy. Except on Sundays. My dad made me go to an hour of Sunday school, an hour and a half of 'adult church', and another hour and fifteen minutes of Sunday night service.

My dad is a Vietnam veteran. A marine. He never talked about his war experiences and it was a family rule that we never, ever shake dad awake. I did ask him once if he had killed anybody in war. He looked at me with his emotionally vacant blue eyes and said, "When it's you or the other guy, you do what you have to do..." Then he spaced out for a moment. I never asked him another question about it. I didn't need to.

If you've ever met a Vietnam vet then you know those guys are messed up. They experienced hell on earth and were not welcomed back as heroes. They generally wear camouflage and have some kind of military insignia on their truck or hats. They wear scraggly facial hair, not the flowing 'make love not war' hippy beards but rugged, hard, gritty facial hair. They tend to be anti-government, anti-social, emotionally unavailable and teach their children to fear God, work hard, and never step out of line or a can of whoop-ass would be opened up on them. My dad and God were very much alike.

The militarized Christianity and version of God I learned early on in my upbringing had a disturbing and profound effect on me. This was a song from my Sunday school. Every kid knew this one:

"Okay children, I want you to sing so loud that the grown-ups can hear you in the sanctuary and don't forget the motions!"

I may never march in the infantry

Ride in the cavalry

Shoot the artillery

I may never fly o'er the enemy

But I'm in the Lord's army!

Yes Sir-re!

I'm in the Lord's army!

Yes sir-re!

I'm in the Lord's army!

Yes sir-re!

Most churches had some sort of training for their youth to insure they grew up knowing their Bible verses and the rights and wrongs of life. AWANA[1] was the most popular youth indoctrination system at the time but our church had something called Olympians. It was similar to a Boy Scouts of America program. There were required weekly tasks, pledges, songs, rituals, awards and patches to mark a young person's progress in the Protestant Christian faith.

In addition to being required to go to church every Wednesday night and twice on Sunday, I also attended revival meetings, missions and evangelism conferences. I wore a young boy's suit, a clip on blue tie and brown cowboy boots—a uniform of sorts. If any of my friends did not show up in the uniform and were able to somehow get away with wearing Wrangler jeans, then they were considered rebels and the parents were in danger of losing their impressionable child to the world rather than the type of nineteen fifties fundamentalist culture that was going on at our church. I always wore the suit to church.

Growing up under the preaching of some of the most scary hell fire and brimstone preachers of the seventies and eighties was spiritually brutal. Although well intentioned, I was groomed for the frontline infantry of the 'Lord's Army' at my local, independent, fundamentalist, inerrant-Bible believing, six literal days of creation, night service required,

---

[1] Awana (derived from the first letters of Approved Workmen Are Not Ashamed as taken from 2 Timothy 2:15) is an international evangelical nonprofit organization founded in 1950. The mission of Awana is to help "churches and parents worldwide raise children and youth to know, love and serve Christ." Awana is a non-denominational program and licenses its curricula to any church willing to pay for and use the Awana materials consistent with its principles.

Baptist church.

Other kids dreamt of bright futures, but my preachers preached constantly about making sure you were saved before the end of the world snuck up on you like a "...thief in the night" (I Thessalonians 5:2). Every bit of news about Israel, communist Russia and the pope haunted my 'end times' doom and gloom future dreams. The rapture[2] that could happen anytime, in the "...twinkling of an eye" (I Corinthians 15:52), would take all of the true believers to heaven and leave unmanned airplanes, trains, and cars crashing into each other. A seven year global tribulation would eventually destroy the earth and His enemies—the nonbelievers in the God of the Bible.

Inside the front cover of every child's Bible was a date. The date was when you were *saved*—when you walked down front during an altar call at the end of the sermon and had asked Jesus to forgive all your sins and to live in your heart. When a good preacher came to visit there would be a line of young people waiting to have the preacher sign their Bibles. I had several preachers sign my Bible. Jack Hyles[3] was my prized

---

[2] The 'rapture' is a teaching extrapolated from different biblical texts claiming that Jesus will come back and rapture up the true believers (universal invisible church) into heaven before the prophecies in the book of Revelation are fulfilled and the ultimate end of the world. John Darby in the 1820-30's popularized this teaching and many claim he invented it.
[3] Jack Hyles (September 25, 1926 – February 6, 2001) was a leading figure in the Independent Baptist movement, having pastored the First Baptist Church of Hammond in Hammond, Indiana, from 1959 until his death. He was also well known for being an innovator of the church bus ministry that brought thousands of people each week from surrounding towns to Hammond for services. Hyles built First to a membership of

signature.

Preachers were my heroes. Sure I liked football and basketball as much as the next kid but preachers, each with their pulpit pounding, sweating brows, tie loosening, and coatthrowing gospel theatrics mesmerized me. They were the voice of God. They were prophets that knew how the world would end. My dad even looked up to these men. I wanted to be one of them.

The other songs I learned as a child mentioned God's love for all the different colored children and how precious they were in His sight, but it was more important that every eight to eighteen year old be saved, baptized, and separated from the worldly society—skeptical of every cultural expression. Everyone needed to be equipped for spiritual warfare by watching the signs of the times in American foreign policy. Everyone needed to be dedicated to daily Bible reading and constantly studying biblical prophecy, ready to quote from the Bible about everyday events. Everyone was at risk of being influenced by the fiery darts of the devil.

As I grew older I learned that the adults on Wednesday night were training to be 'prayer warriors'. They constantly prayed for our church members to not get sick, the youth not to get caught in sins, like smoking, drinking or sneaking to the movies. Everyone begged God to be blessed and maintain a middle class lifestyle, or keep a job, and always be a good

<hr>

100,000 making it the most attended Baptist church in the United States. He was accused of several controversies while pastoring the church, and his doctrinal positions often put him at odds with other Christians — even with other fundamentalist Baptists.

witness to any unsaved people they knew.

Every year there would be two conferences. One was a mission's conference. I was taught to pray for the lost people of India, Africa, China, Russia and Catholics. We would pledge as a family to give money to missionaries around the world who believed and taught the Bible the same way our church did. There were even flags of all the countries around our auditorium that our church sponsored. Missionaries were special and honored greatly by the posting of their family pictures on postcards (called prayer cards) on everybody's refrigerators.

I heard the missionaries' stories. On their furloughs they traveled the fundamentalist Bible-believing church circuit. They talked of setting up base camps in the dangerous jungles. They talked of warring tribes and trying to explain salvation and the Bible to cannibals. They told their stories and reported the number of souls saved, then asked for money and prayers. It sounded horrible, a beggars life and a sure way to die for your faith. I did not want to go to Africa and live out in a hut and risk being speared by a vengeful pigmy. They were surely doing the work of God as field soldiers, but it lacked the celebrity and excitement of the traveling preacher.

The second annual conference was about the book of Revelation and the end times. Preachers would come in with maps and charts and stories to scare the hell out of every man, woman, and child. We were in a war for the souls of every lost person. It was a race against time for those souls because the rapture could happen at any moment. I sat in the front of every one of those conferences with my church friends, not by choice mind you but by command. This was serious business and we were the next generation of the Lord's army.

The preachers warned us that the enemy combatants lurked in every institution in the world. American Christians were in a spiritual and cultural war and had several active frontlines engaged in hostile fighting: Jerry Falwell was the general in charge of the political battlefront leading his Moral Majority. Bob Jones University was the last bunker of the 'separate but equal' racial gospel culture division. Billy Graham was the crusader with his cavalry of the *Four Horsemen of the Apocalypse* galloping across America. Francis Schaeffer made propaganda films against the higher educated liberals, and Jack Van Impie lead the elite scouting brigade, always watching the papacy and clues in the news about the coming rapture, seven year tribulation and the final battle of Armageddon.

Our enemies were many: Atheists, gays, the left over drug addicted hippies of the sixties, baby killing Democrats, communist Russia lead by Mikhail Gorbachev, the possible antichrist, with the mark of the beast on his forehead, the hedonistic Hollywood elites, the clandestine secular humanists employed by every college or university that did not have the word 'Bible' in its name, tag line, or fight song.

Our allies if you could call them that, were untrustworthy: Snake-handling Pentecostals were emotionally disillusioned and misinterpreted the Bible concerning 'speaking in tongues' and Holy Spirit healings. They also danced in the aisles to an oxymoron called 'praise rock' music. The Calvinists were on the other side, too rational and smug in their status of being the *Elect*. They constantly worked over the variations of the Five Points of Calvinism[4] and were more concerned with theology than straight Bible reading and application. The mainline denominations were closet liberals standing at their pulpits wearing colorful gender confusing robes. The Catholics were traitors. They believed their works would save them, plus, they worshiped tiny little idols of the Virgin Mary enshrined in half buried bathtubs all over the city.

Unity with other Christians depended on whether they used the King James version only, how they interpreted the prophetic timeline for the end of the world, worshipped, and how literal they applied the Bible. Our church wouldn't even play softball against non-Baptist churches. No other church was a true ally. No one fully agreed with anyone, not pastors with biblical scholars, not assistant pastors with pastors, deacon boards with the congregations, worship leaders with choirs, youth pastors with adult leaders, Sunday school teachers with families. Eventually every person became an *Army of One*, yet somehow all of the different Protestant churches were considered a unified body of believers called

---

[4] The acronym **TULIP** summarizes the core of Reformed Theology- Man is **Totally Depraved**, God **Unconditionally Elects** some for salvation, consequently there is **Limited Atonement** made for only the Elect, **Irresistible Grace** assures that the Elect will respond to their true status as Elect and **Perseverance** of the saints teaches that God's salvific purpose cannot be thwarted for the Elect. There is a continuum of differing definitions and understandings of TULIP.

the *Church militant*[5]—the Lord's army.

I was taught and trained to use the ultimate weapon in our war with everyone. It was not some red button on a nuclear submarine off the coast of the eastern Atlantic Ocean. It was a thumb on the concordance of the King James Bible. In Sunday school we played a game called 'Sword Drill'. The youth pastor would tell us to raise our Bibles in the air. Then he would call out a verse, twice, then yell, "Go!" All the youth then would frantically flip the Bible open and search for the verse. The first person to find it would stand up and blurt out what the verse read. I was pretty quick at the sword drill. I got really good with my sword, my Bible, my weapon.

The Bible was "... sharper than any two edged sword" (Hebrews 4:12). The inerrant, literal interpretation, King James Version was the final authority concerning God and Christian life. A culturally separate, Republican minded, middle class American standard of living, and Protestant dispensational theology[6] were the lenses used to apply this manual for the Christian life.

It was the perfect weapon and could be used by anyone. My preacher heroes used it with great effect on me and everyone agreed with the need to spread the Word at every opportunity, in every medium, and in every place you could.

---

[5] The term *Church militant* refers to Christians currently alive on earth; compared to the term *Church triumphant* made up of Christians who have died.

[6] Dispensational theology views biblical history as a series of dispensations, or separated time-periods, with each dispensation in the Bible representing a different way in which God reveals Himself to man.

At every stage of growing up my given mission was to slip in a Bible verse like a 'micky-finn' wherever and however I could.

I openly challenged the science teacher about evolution in 7th grade biology class with an assault of verses from Genesis. I even wrote Bible verses in the text book. I left Bible tracks on urinals, in secular books at bookstores, and I always had a couple within reach ready to give to a stranger at a moment's notice, when the Spirit moved me to do so.

'You may be the only Bible someone reads' became everyone's personal responsibility. I was indoctrinated, brainwashed, to believe the end of the world was right around the corner and everyone's eternal destiny was somehow my responsibility and would be my fault if I failed in this mission: Save the lost at all costs.

I was taught how to pick the right bumper stickers for our American made cars, how to get people saved, go to church every Sunday and vote Republican based on their foreign policy and love for Israel.

I was taught to be ready for another holocaust. Only this time it would be the whole world against true Bible believing Christians, against us at our little fundamentalist church, against me, a poor son of a vet growing up in a dilapidated cottage on a lake.

My church taught me to fear God, work hard, and never step out of line or a divine can of whoop-ass would be opened up on me. Although I would never have the chance to be a solider, like my dad, I knew I could win his approval and God's approval if I fought valiantly in the Lord's army. If we really were getting ready for an apocalyptic end time war, like the preachers preached, and if it was going to come down to me or the other guy; then this son of a vet was going to do what he had to do.

r. leo olson

PREACHER BOY

"Okay children, I want you to sing it again, but sing it so loud that the grown-ups in the sanctuary can hear you."

The B-I-B-L-E
Yes, that's the book for me
I stand alone on the Word of God
The B-I-B-L-E...Bible!

Looking back I realize this song was a lie. It was also the cause of my spiritual head injuries. In this seemingly little harmless rhyme lives a spiritual cancer and the most spiritually injurious weapon of mass destruction to my soul.

I interpreted God's authoritative Word alone but applied it to everybody else's life. It was amazing how easy it was to apply my Bible readings and applications to other people. And when I spoke up at school against secular teachings, tried to save my Catholic friends or put Bible verses on my school folders I was praised as being 'on fire' for the Lord—'You're a special young man of God, *anointed* with a gift of the Holy Spirit.'

It felt good to be thought of as special and it gave me temporary relief from the hypocrisy of no longer being able to apply or obey what I read in the Bible personally when I wasn't at church. Yet I didn't stop requiring it of others. I believed I was becoming a prophet, a true voice of the Lord even with this duality of roles growing inside of me.

I played this 'specially anointed' role up in front of adults and at youth group but another version of me existed at school and with my non-church friends—a wilder, more sinful pleasure seeking role. Most people have moments when they behave like sinners and behave like saints, but I played both roles at the same time—a true spiritually schizophrenic split.

I justified, enjoyed and was opportunistic using both versions of myself to deal with my irreconcilable fears of not being worthy of heaven, yet not wanting to spend eternity in hell. Honestly, neither looked like a fun place to spend eternity but as long as the two versions of me didn't overlap I thought I could even fool God. I thought He was in desperate need of preachers and evangelists because He had a history of using sinners to do great things, like King David, Paul and Peter.

This especially gifted *'anointing'* I was supposed to have gave me a status promotion. At fifteen years old, I was promoted to a *special forces* team called the 'preacher boys'. Despite the decade of constant preaching about how sinful I was and how I could do nothing to save my soul or self-esteem from hell except believe a simple formula of salvation,[7] I signed up. Being a preacher boy gave me another role to play and hopefully would create another, better version of myself.

The more articulate boys, which I was one of, were chosen and trained for the frontlines to preach the Word of God and save souls by assassinating the sinful devilish influences in a persons' life. "For the wages of sin is death, but the gift of God is eternal life" (Romans 6:23). We were evaluated to see if our style was more like General Falwell, Graham, Schaeffer or Van Impe.

Our adult leaders or sergeants would mine old copies of a fundamentalist Christian newspaper called, *The Sword of the Lord* for sermons by fire and brimstone preachers. They would edit and cut the sermons down to three points and offer the same emotionally manipulative 'altar call' ending:

> Can I have every head bowed and every eye closed?
> Now if you would like to receive Jesus as your per-
> sonal Savior today, please raise your hand. I'll come
> talk to you about it after the sermon. Anyone at all?
> No one is looking. If the Holy Spirit is talking to

---

[7] This formula or mental transactional belief of salvation detailed how much Christ had to suffer a gruesome, bloody death in a most horrible crucifixion to appease His wrathful and eternally pissed off Father because of my personal sins. It required to me to **Admit** I was a sinner, **Believe** Jesus died for those sins in my place, and **Confess** Him as Lord and Savior by asking him to live in my heart. **A-B-C**. See substitutionary or vicarious atonement.

you in that still small voice right now, just raise your hand. Don't say 'no' to God. This might be your last chance to accept the gospel for we don't know when our life will be required of us. I believe the Lord is speaking to someone today. Is it you? Just raise your hand.

I was trained to first get people to understand they were *lost*. The lost were sinners in the hands of an angry God who hated sin and were in danger of hell. Then when they were hopeless, self-condemned and with heads bowed and eyes closed, I could *save* them—get them to believe a simple message of salvation. Why would anyone want to go to hell when going to heaven is so easy? The ultimate goal of a preacher boy was to be cultivated and drafted as part of the next generation of preachers who would save the lost. So we were taught to role play, preach with emotion, and conjure up moments for life changing salvation decisions.

We were given these revamped sermons and told to memorize them, internalize them, and infuse them with fist pounding Bible waving theatrics. When the guest preachers would come to visit for a revival or conference, the preacher boys were watching every move, every motion, every dramatic pause so we could hone our own skills.

My favorite move was when the preacher would take off his suit coat, slowly roll up his sleeves while his words were building with emotion. He would then take off his watch and put in on the pulpit and then, *wham*, he would pound the pulpit and yell out a command like repent! What power.

What conviction. And that amazingly long finger that pointed at everyone and no one at the same time. I used to practice that move all the time but never was able to give the finger to my listeners the same way they could.

We were training for a local, regional, and national competition where preacher boys from all over would compete in spiritual blood sport. The really good preacher boys got at least someone to raise their hand during the competition or it wasn't good enough preaching to win.

So at the end of my junior year in high school I stood in a classroom at Grand Rapids School of Bible and Music, pounded the lectern, and tried to call the fire of heaven down on sinful lost souls like Elijah of old.[8] The three stoic judges rated my performance on twenty eight different factors on a scale of one to ten including introduction, content, delivery, application and closing gospel invitation. I preached my ass off, and even though no one raised a hand at my altar call ending, I pretended someone did to score higher with the judges, and said, "Thank you, I see that hand." That year, I advanced to regionals and then to the national competition held during a summer camp at Word of Life Bible Institute in Schroon Lake New York. This place was where your future value as an all-star preacher could be discovered, like a Christian talent show for independent fundamentalist Bible believing churches across America.

During the summer, when school was out, I still had to keep up appearances in both worlds; bon-fires and peach

---

[8] Ref. I Kings 18

schnapps on Saturday nights and grape juice with communion crackers on Sunday nights.

Three days before I left for that national competition I cried myself to sleep, begging God to forgive me and was seriously fearful of going to hell because I had gone too far with a girl on the porch on Saturday night.

My hormones and my preacher boy image were at war within me. I was having a hard time keeping the two versions of myself separate. I didn't want to preach. I wasn't worthy. I wanted to just be sent to hell and get it over with. But I also wanted to be used by God, make Him happy with me. Let Him know I was at least trying with one version of myself. I needed a divine intervention. So I preached.

I won first place for the second time in my life. Out of the entire nation of Bible believing churches, I was the number one preacher boy. I wondered if it was a sign that God had forgiven me of my sins and blessed me with winning a spiritual contest. I wondered if this was what it was like to be in the Lord's army and stand alone on the B-I-B-L-E.

Onward Christian Soldier
Onward, Christian soldiers, marching as to war,
With the cross of Jesus going on before.
Christ, the royal Master, leads against the foe;
Forward into battle see His banners go!
Onward, Christian soldiers, marching as to war,
With the cross of Jesus going on before...

THE WAGER

My duplicitous spiritual schizophrenia had reached its peak when I was a senior in high school. I was a two time national preacher boy champion but I also had an all-American high school experience—captain of a conference champion football team, on the homecoming court, muscularly fit, funny, voted the class flirt, and partied like a rock star. After graduation, I planned to go to Central Michigan University for more of the same.

On Saturday nights I would make it home minutes before curfew and flop on my bed, room spinning from the bon fire peach schnapps buzz I had. I tried not to look at my desk, where the awards for winning those preaching contests were displayed next to a thick, black, gold-leafed King James Bible and something called a Quiet Time Diary. The QT Diary contained a couple of verses from the Bible and a place to write what the verses meant and how one should apply them to his life.

The summer before, my parents had read that diary and confronted me about my diary sins. I then used that diary as propaganda for counter intelligence—to keep them from knowing what I was really doing with my life. I had a 'boom box' and a stack of Christian rock cassettes. The only church approved music for a teenager was a hymn singing a capella group named Glad. My parents were more liberal, they let me listen to DC Talk, Carmen and somehow I snuck in Erasure.[9] In my closet hung my Sunday suit. Every Sunday I would put it on for the church service and then take it off and hang it up again in the closet for the rest of the week, just like my Christianity. The other version of me started to hate the suit.

I didn't sleep well back then. Maybe it was the emptiness I felt inside, or the monstrous guilt trip I heard with every Sunday sermon, or the quiet fear I held in my heart that maybe the formula for salvation didn't take for me—but a stone was in my spiritual shoe and disrupting my trophy winning spiritually duplicitous self.

I got up one night and went to sit at the end of a dock on the lake we lived on. It was a clear fall night. The moon was full, the stars were particularly bright, even shining off the still-glass like water.

I was so sad. I had a wonderful, promising, hedonistically pleasurable life ahead of me and yet I was shackled with fear of hell, guilt, a bloody mental picture of Christ and spiritual melancholy.[10] I didn't pray much. Prayer was only utilitari-

---

[9] A 1985 openly gay European New Wave, synth-pop music duo.

[10] The dominate word picture in sermons was a bloody Jesus Christ on a cross. Every day I read, saw a picture, or heard about bloody Jesus. The suffering of Christ on the cross for my personal sins was the theme of many hymns like 'Victory in Jesus' or 'There is Power in the Blood'. The hyper exaltation and explanations of the violence of crucifixion was readily available. As a young person I carried notes from a sermon in my Bible which detailed a medical analysis of a crucifixion. Eventually, I was

an—a crutch for me to relieve a constant guilt in my soul, or to ask to win another preaching contest. God wasn't real to me except when I needed Him.

I'm not sure where this irreverent boldness came from that arose inside of me, but I raised my fist to the sky that night and said something like this:

> Alright, I'll make a deal with you God. I will give you one year of my life. I'll do whatever you want me to do, as long as you make it clear. If you love me, have really saved me and this Christian life is all it's cracked up to be, then make me a believer. I can always wear the suit on Sunday, win a preaching contest from time to time and keep on with the party life I have now. But you have to make it clear, no guessing and you only get one year.

I made a wager with God. I was taught God hated gambling but what the hell did I have to lose?

I lowered my fist and stared at the moon. I wanted a sign, an omen, a 'peace that passed all understanding',[11] a fish to jump or something, but there was no magic sign that night. My terms of the wager were non-negotiable, one year and

---

desensitized and I stopped feeling anything when I saw or heard about the sufferings of Christ.

[11] "Be anxious for nothing, but in everything by prayer and supplication, with thanksgiving, let your requests be made known to God; and the peace of God, which surpasses all understanding, will guard your hearts and minds through Christ Jesus" (Philippians 4:6-8).

unmistakably clear direction or party time at Central Michigan University and football try-outs.

For months there was only divine silence and devilish fun. It was Sunday and I put the suit on. *I don't think I ever dry cleaned that thing in all the years I wore it.* I only wore it Sunday mornings from ten until twelve thirty and if I preached—it was gray.

There were some college students from our congregation on winter break from Word of Life Bible Institute. They were given the opportunity to share about their time at WOLBI (pronounced: waul-bee) and what they had learned. The speakers were mainly girls.

These were the older girls from my church that I had crushes on for years. They were good girls, beautiful and nice, 'church' girls that only saw my Sunday suit version. However, as they each got up to share their testimony, they kept using a phrase over and over again: 'It will be the best year of your life.'

I talked to one of the visiting co-eds, the prettiest one of course, after the service and questioned her enthusiasm about this one year at Word of Life Bible Institute. She was infectious and filled with something inside her soul that I did not have.

"You will not regret it. It's only one year and then you'll have a biblical foundation for the rest of your life. You should go; give one year of your life to God," she said, hugged me and walked away.

I walked out to my red beater car, a Monza Spyder, and held the steering wheel and said out loud, "Well, that was pretty clear, a little eerie, but clear. Okay, I'll go." I went home and told my parents that I would like to go to WOLBI before I go to Central Michigan. They were over-joyed, like the prodigal son had finally come home. I thought I had fooled them all this time but the joy on their faces proved they had been worried.

∞

I finished my second semester of my senior year with hope that God was really directing my life. He gave me a sign to go to Word of Life. I was preaching again and I thought He was still going to use me in some big way despite the wreckage of hypocrisy caused by my double life. I tried to focus my efforts and battle the injuries caused by abusing my body with alcohol, a reckless partying reputation and objectifying others for sinful pleasure. I excused it as 'sowing my wild oats' until I read Galatians 6:7-8a in my QT Diary, 'Do not be deceived, God is not mocked; for whatever a man sows, that he will also reap. For he who sows to his flesh will of the flesh reap corruption.'

These kinds of injuries were self-inflicted and I realized I had injured others too. I felt tremendous guilt every time I had a quiet moment to myself. I knew I had to memorialize the wounded of my other life—move on, but carry them in my memory forever. I had made a wager and now had to try and wear the gray suit all the time.

I had a new Christian girlfriend who did not go to my church or my school and did not know the extent of my spiritual schizophrenia. My parents backed off spying because

I was now going to a Bible college. I tried to focus on my 'church life' and being the best preacher boy in the nation.

∞

The preaching competition in my senior year was tough going. A friend named Pierce was last year's junior high preacher boy champion and he was gunning for me. I made it to nationals again. Pierce and I were the front runners in the whole competition. He was good but I was the reigning preacher boy champion and the odds on favorite to win it again.

On the bus ride to the national competition I sat and starred with empty eyes at my reflection in the window as the bus rhythmically drummed to upstate New York. I was a proud preacher boy on the outside but a severely injured child tormented by a duplicitous spiritual schizophrenia on the inside—preacher boy and party boy.

I missed my drinking friends, the girls at bon fires and the excitement of Friday night. I wanted to really change on the inside but was seduced back from time to time. I was running with the devil and still trying to walk with the Lord. I read my Bible and prayed every day, except Friday and Saturdays. I wanted to repent, be transformed, sanctified, justified, glorified and all those other theological terms I had heard preached. I truly wanted to leave behind the other me but that guy was so fun to hang out with. I was in the snares of the devil. The preacher seemed to be preaching directly to me every Sunday. I was soul sick and contaminated others in the guise of young love and Friday night fun. I wanted God to forgive and forget but I didn't know if I could forgive or forget myself or if anyone else could. There was an inner war going on inside me. I would read Romans chapter 7 over and over and thought Paul had the same thing going on when he said he wanted to do good but couldn't.[12] It helped me feel a little better about myself because he was an apostle struggling with this stuff and I was only a preacher boy.

But I wanted some assurance that God would really forgive me and was going to heal me and take care of the others I'd wounded. The guilt was crushing me and I had no relief. I felt like there was no room for me to breathe spiritually. I knew I needed to suck it up and perform my preaching to the best of my ability. I promised God on that bus ride that I would leave behind all my sinful ways, once and for all and never question His forgiveness again if He let me win this time too. It was tear-filled prayerful bargaining. I needed to win that preaching contest to be assured that God had forgiven my multitude of sins and was going to still honor His end of our wager— that the Christian life was all it was cracked up to be. He did this deal the year before when I had won; I kept reminding myself.

So there I stood up in front of several hundred teens, parents and event organizers with my spiritual life in the balance. The title of my sermon was *Sin - The Problem and The Solution*.

---

[12] "For the good that I will to do, I do not do; but the evil I will not to do, that I practice" (Romans 7:19).

I opened with a story about a poisonous plant in Brazil called the 'murderer vine' that grew slowly around a tree until it eventually killed the tree. My four points were: What is sin? What kind of sin might a person commit? What does God think of sin? And my closing invitation was: What can you do about sin? I concluded with a threat of burning in hell where the fire is never quenched and unrepentant sinners are tormented forever. The only choice was to confess your sins, ask Jesus in your heart and accept the free gift of salvation paid for by Jesus on a bloody cross or burn in hell forever. You may die in a car ride on the way home, I warned in my concluding 'altar call', so make sure you know beyond a shadow of a doubt where you will be one second after you die.

I walked off the stage to thunderous applause. I had performed my special gift to my best. I thought I was a lock to win it all and be forgiven of all my 'wild oat sowing' sins.

I came in second behind Pierce. I was happy for him, not jealous at all. Pierce and I were fine with each other but I wondered about God and me. We went home and were both greeted by our church as co-victors and ready for battle in the real world. Our spoils were an opportunity to preach our sermons during the evening service. I went first and like a true biblical assassin pointed my finger at the congregation and fired my shots about sin and God's hatred for it. Someone yelled, "Amen" and I smiled because that was equivalent to the Marine Corps marksmanship medal. Every preacher boy wanted a real 'amen'.

Nobody raised their hand to be saved that night. Nobody

was moved to repent or amend their life. Nobody was encouraged to love their neighbor. Everyone applauded and when I sat down with the other teens in the front row, an adult leaned forward and whispered in my ear, "You should have won."

I wasn't sure if God had forgiven me or not. I didn't win. God had kept His part of the wager about giving clear directions for the next step in my life but I didn't win. It wasn't clear to me where He and I stood about forgiveness, so I applied and was accepted to Central Michigan University as a backup in case God backed out. I debated about going to Word of Life many nights on that dock but I knew in my heart that I had to go—I owed God a year.

r. leo olson

BIBLICAL ASSASSIN BOOT CAMP

'Way up high in the Adirondack Mountains' nestled on the shores of another lake is where I would fulfill my wager with God. There is no place on God's green earth like Word of Life Bible Institute.[13]

Word of Life 'Bridal' Institute or 'Find a wife at Word of Life' are the two unofficial slogans of the Institute, although marriage was strictly prohibited by registered students. WOLBI consisted of 800 to 1800 students any given year. The demographics were mainly high school grads from America's independent, fundamentalist, fire and brimstone preaching, literal interpretation of the Bible, Baptist-type churches. There were some older people trying to get into a ministry or training to be missionaries but mainly it was this

---

[13] I could write a whole separate volume about my time at Word of Life Bible Institute. I could skew my memories negative or positive concerning WOLBI but that would be unfair, for I have mixed feelings about it. I liked every person there. I have a dear friend who has since converted to Judaism because of her time there and I have another friend that gave his whole life to that Institute and ran sister Institutes in Europe. I have kept them in my prayers to this very day. One rejected Jesus as God and the other is radically devoted to Him. I think that is so curious. This chapter records my experiences there twenty plus-years ago concerning its unique culture.

group of hormonally suppressed youth that God had chosen for me to live out my one year wager.

There was a code of conduct that removed all worldly distractions—no music, no TV, no magazines, no personal phones, no movies, no drinking, no smoking, no unapproved books, no card playing, no privacy, no masturbating and no physical touching of any kind with the opposite sex, none. ('you must always leave room for the Holy Spirit') This code of conduct was cited with Bible verses and the spiritual reasoning behind each rule. Although adherence to the rules was not to be considered a measuring stick of 'spirituality' anything but cheerful obedience would be considered sinful disobedience and a spiritual problem.

This 'chapter and verse' referenced code of conduct, with a two page detailed dress code, and the scheduling of every minute of the day was the only way for the Institute to maintain order and systematically indoctrinate the next generation of the Lord's army. When I think about it now, it was really the only way to manage that many horny eighteen year olds from so many fundamentalist Bible believing churches, where rule keeping was how to define our 'walk with the Lord'. The administration and resident assistants were told to be strict and try to make it 'not' about the rules. However it was always about the 'rules' and the methodology of using the Bible to rationalize, defend, and enforce them that solidified a most injurious and performance based spirituality for me.

Ask any good ol'Bible banging church goer, 'How do you know if a young person is 'walking with the Lord'? The answer will quickly be described two-fold; a life style of social separation condemning the evil world of higher education, Democratic politics and Hollywood entertainment; and secondly, conformity to a militaristic bend of literal biblical applications often with 'end times' nuances, heavy local church attendance, supporting a Christian right-Zionist-Republican political agenda and the endless evaluations of a proper Christian lifestyle when it comes to entertainment, literature, music and art.[14]

This place, for me, was like a biblical boot camp. Like a Christian Citadel with its three core values. First, the curriculum was a systematic indoctrination of the literal interpretation of the Bible. The Bible served as the foundation for all educational disciplines and trumped any scientific, psychological, archeological, philosophical or historical conflicting claims. Second, a strict obedience to its applications in all areas of life defined the 'right' kind of church and Christians you could associate with. Third, a biblical proof-texted confrontational gospel message and strategy for saving the lost, hell bound, people of the world. God wants you to turn or burn, baby. Give me a Marine Corp hoo-raah!

When not in class or doing your campus job you would have the opportunity to put all this biblical knowledge into practice. There were teams of people that would go to the big cities and stand on a box and preach the salvific formula of 'confess your sins, accept Christ's death on the cross as payment for such sins, then ask Jesus in your heart so you can

---

[14] For further reading search: Dominionism

go to heaven instead of burning in hell. It was called 'Open-Air Campaigning'. It was like that guy at large festivals or public gatherings who carries an eight foot cross, dressed as a bloody Christ, with another guy on a mega phone telling people to repent or go to hell—except no cross or fake blood.

There were other fun ministries too. There was summer camp where you could be a counselor and save young souls before they messed up their lives with rock music, heavy petting or going to the movies. Or prison ministry, which I did—there is nothing quite like an eighteen year old quoting the Bible and preaching to violent criminals—fun times.

In the Marine Corp all new recruits learn the Rifleman's Creed penned by Major General William Henry Rupertus:

This is my **rifle**. There are many like it, but this one is mine.

My **rifle** is my best friend. It is my life. I must master it as I must master my life.

My **rifle**, without me, is useless. Without my **rifle**, I am useless. I must fire my **rifle** true. I must shoot straighter than my enemy who is trying to kill me. I must shoot him before he shoots me. I will...

My **rifle** and myself know that what counts in this war is not the rounds we fire, the noise of our burst, nor the smoke we make. We know that it is the hits that count. We will hit...

My **rifle** is human, even as I, because it is my life. Thus, I will learn it as a brother. I will learn its weaknesses, its strength, its parts, its accessories, its sights and its barrel. I will ever guard it against the ravages of weather and damage as I will ever guard my legs, my arms, my eyes and my heart against damage. I will keep my **rifle** clean and ready. We will become part of each other. We will...

Before God, I swear this creed. My **rifle** and my-self are the defenders of my country. We are the masters of our enemy. We are the saviors of my life.

So be it, until victory is America's and there is no enemy, but peace!

If you substitute **Bible** for **rifle** in the creed above you will understand what happened to me at Word of Life Bible Institute. I became a biblical assassin. It didn't happen to everyone, some became 'liberal' Christians at best and Catholics at worst but not me—not someone who had wagered his life for one year to learn about the Christian life worth living. I bought into it all; it was God's will, God's word and God's warning—save the lost at all cost.

My weapon became my King James Version Bible, black leather, underlined everywhere with all the 'thee's' and 'thou's' that added the exploding tips to my ammunition of 'chapter and verse' total proof texting recall. It was gold leafed with two blood red ribbon page markers (rifle sites), but no finger indent tabs—those Bibles were for wussies, coast guard Christians. I was a Navy Seal, Green Beret, an Army Ranger.

Yep, I bought into the whole thing and didn't have any hints that something was wrong until I came back from winter break. The code of conduct from the student manual was on a separate sheet of paper and handed out at the first class. The administration asked every student to sign his name stating that he had kept the code of conduct over the winter break.

I had not. I listened to a mixed tape of Depeche Mode, The Cure and OMD, (C'mon it was the nineties) I cuddled and kissed my girlfriend while watching a movie the last night of break and I learned to play euchre with her parents.

Yes, I played cards with those evil satanically symbolic cards—the suicide king of hearts with a sword in his head, the whore of Babylon looking queen of hearts and their obviously gay looking, thin handle bar mustached, bastard jack of hearts. As if these obviously perverted mock theologies weren't warning enough, playing cards could easily lead to gambling, drinking, dancing, adultery, orgies, deviant and experimental bi-curious sex, eventually sex with monkeys and then AIDS— God's punishment for homosexuality according to the prevailing biblical teaching of the times.

Now I had done many sins in my life. I was no saint but I

never flat out lied. I had kept vital information from people before and had been 'Clintonesque' by being intentionally ambiguous with the meaning of words—but to bold face lie; I can't do that. The guilt is too much for me to bear and I come clean with the smallest of pressure. So I did not sign the sheet.

A few days later I was given a note stating that the dean of students would like to see me about why I had not signed the code of conduct sheet. I was to report that afternoon during the hour and forty five minutes of free time in the schedule.

I walked up to the administration offices and signed in on a clip board and waited in the lobby with the other guilt ridden sinners. A young girl came out crying, her face was blotchy. I wondered what her sin was. Then a guy came out crying. I wondered what the hell was going on behind that door. I vowed not to cry as my turn was next.

I walked in and sat down across from the dean. To my right was a large book case of theological books and Bible commentaries. To my left, hanging on the wall were several degrees from universities and on the large desk with stacks of ungraded test papers and essays sat a man that was like God the judge. I wanted to cry.

"So Mr. Olson, you were not able to sign the code of conduct sheet. Can you tell me why?"

I had never told anyone my sins before or went to any type of confession. I didn't need to.[15] My sins were confessed into my pillow at night. I had a lump in my throat, my mouth was

---

[15] "For there is one God and one Mediator between God and men, the Man Christ Jesus" (I Timothy 2:5).

dry and I could not look him in the eyes. I saw the Catholics go to confession in movies but that was in adjoined closets with a screen separating the priest and sinner. Every effort for anonymity was kept. I am sitting in front of the man who would send me home if I had broken too many of the rules. *If that happened what would God do with my wager? Give up on me because I couldn't follow the rules? Send me to hell?* I was scared and felt so small in that chair, I was on the judgment seat. I really wanted to cry now.

I thought about pleading ignorance and that I didn't know I was to keep all the rules of Word of Life at home—that wouldn't work, lie upon lie. I wanted to rationalize that the stringent rules of the Institute were not the same rules of my church or my personal convictions—in other words, they were not sins. I thought about a lot of things I could say in that moment while he waited me out. The guilt crushed me and I squirmed in my seat.

Finally, I blurted as fast as I could, "I have a girlfriend that I love and I was affectionate with her—didn't have sex but...I watched a movie, listened to rock music and I played cards with her parents and it was all fun and I don't count any of them as sins but now that you hold this code of conduct over my head I feel like I have sinned. I don't agree with any of this and if you want to send me home then I guess that is what you should do."

I was on the verge of tears just like the other rebels that had sat in my seat minutes earlier. I had never stood up to a spiritual authority like that in my life, except shaking my fist at God on the dock, but this was different. You can't see God and He generally gave me the silent treatment anyway.

The dean turned out to be very gracious and calm. He warned me of the dangers of pre-marital affection and how it can lead to fornication. He told me that Lucifer was in charge of music in Heaven and now uses rock music to wage a war on the mind of Christians—he asked me if I ever wondered why those songs stuck in my head so easily and yet it's so hard to memorize Scripture. I had not thought of this before. But he spent most of his time explaining the associated evilness of card playing and how it was a doorway to the darker sinful sides of life.

The whole thing reminded me of two movies I was allowed to see as a child. One was Star Wars. The other was a b-grade movie[16] I saw when I was ten, about a sinful motorcycle gang rider that drank, smoked and played cards. A clean cut white guy encouraged him to ask Jesus in his heart and be saved from his sinful life and an eternity in hell. He chose to wait and continue on with his sinful life towards the *dark side of the force*. He crashed on the way home one night from a party and awoke in a place he didn't recognize. Demonic creatures with gold hair, human faces, and animal bodies heckled him. He sat down next to the devil at a camp fire and the devil told him he was dead and in hell. The man jumped up and dropped his helmet on the ground. It rolled around and revealed his own head in the helmet, just like Luke Skywalker when he faced his fears in the Dagobah system in

---

[16] A Thief in the Night is a 1972 Christian 'end times' film produced by Russell S. Doughten.

<u>Return of the Jedi</u> when under Vader's helmet revealed Luke's own face. The man with the axe, the king of diamonds, had got the motorcycle rider. Maybe the dean was right. Maybe the dean was my Yoda and he was telling me to use the good side of the force.

The lump in my throat weakened and I had unclenched my fists the more he talked. I didn't agree with him but he made the point that I had voluntarily enrolled in the Institute and I should make every effort to abide by the rules not because I agreed with them but because it was a matter of integrity and character and sacrifice of freedom for the 'weaker' brothers among us. I never knew playing cards was so evil.

I bought this line of reasoning and left the office without tears. I walked down the paved hill past my dorm room. I felt something in my heart after talking to him but didn't know what it was.

Snow blanketed everything and I thought about the verse that says our sins are like scarlet and as red as crimson but He has made them as white as snow.[17] I wanted to feel like I had been forgiven. But did God forgive me for playing cards? Or did the dean forgive me? Something was manufactured about the whole thing. It was this place, these rules, this type of spirituality that had caused this pseudo-repentance in my soul. I looked into the eyes of my classmates for any glimpse of authentic repentance, humility, joy or realness. I saw only fear, guilt or glassy-eyed obedience—conforming clones.

---

[17] "...though your sins are like scarlet, they shall be as white as snow..." (Isaiah 1:18).

Everyone outwardly went along with everything—played the role and acted the part. It was the first of many 'disconnects' and contradictions I would experience in this tradition of Christianity—this spirituality.

I was now in a place where I was not the same person I was in high school and not doing the same things, but the same core sins were there—being suppressed outwardly. I had even more emptiness and guilt because now I was 'acting' like a good Christian. I now wore the Sunday suit every day but remained just as fake. I wondered if this was all there was to the Christian life that I wagered for.

I was still so sad, confused and spiritually injured inside but what could one young person do? Challenge a whole school that only existed to teach the Bible? I conformed too and threw myself into learning everything I could about the Bible for this one year. After all, this was where God had clearly led me in my wager.

However, the next day I went to my dorm mate and asked him to shave my head, military style. It was my silent protest. I did not receive one demerit, aced every test, achieved honors status, did my campus job with excellence every time and obeyed every rule the rest of my time at Word of Life. I was the perfect Christian, on the outside.

Maybe this was the Christian life worth living. If I just conformed to the biblical rules then I would be okay with God. The Old Testament was full of rules and maybe that's all there was to the Christian life until the Lord came back. I resolved that I was the only person who felt like something was wrong. I certainly couldn't offer an alternative view of spirituality so I must have been just really messed up inside.

I started to look for a sign—another 'clear' direction from God, a fish to jump, another message from a beautiful church girl or something. There was this older mentally unstable man, named Gene that sat by me in a class. He would sneak a couple of puffs on a cigarette in between classes—*sinner, he broke the code of conduct during class breaks.*

I followed him outside one day. He was moving between trees trying to be unseen. I meandered after him, posing to go by the lake. After several moments of him not being able to shake me; he walked purposefully up to me, crazy look in his eyes and handed me a piece of paper with a verse from Revelation on it.

"I only have a short time here, maybe this is why God sent me here—to give you this message," he said then darted off to get his nicotine fix.

A clear sign! A verse in Hebrews came immediately to my mind—"Do not forget to entertain strangers, for by so doing some have unwittingly entertained angels" (Hebrews 13:2). *Was Gene my angel in disguise? Can angels smoke?* I didn't care.

I hustled back and looked up the verse from the book of Revelation. The verse had no obvious meaning; it was a transition verse from one chapter to another. He was on a mission from God with verses that he gave meaning to in his own little Christian world. Was this whole place making little Gene's? Was I becoming a mentally unstable Gene type of Christian? Would I start smoking now? Maybe the message was that another transition was about to come. I wasn't sure of anything anymore. I was a loaded gun of biblical bullets and deep inside no longer trusted my drill sergeants, pastors or hot church girls who talked about the best year of their lives.

∞

For the summer, WOLBI students were required to do a ministry internship in order to complete the education and earn a diploma. Almost everyone becomes a camp counselor to help run their thriving summer camp ministry. But I had to get out of that place so I begged to go home for a local church ministry internship. It was granted against all protocols.

I took it as a sign from God that I was ready to serve the Lord in the real world. I was a champion preacher boy, honors student at a Bible college, quick witted and had an almost instant recall memory of the Bible. I could save souls at a moment's notice and with sniper precision could tell other Christians where their lives didn't match up with the Bible's teaching.

It was at home that I put these sniper assassination skills to work. My victims were everyone who did not agree with the Bible as I was taught it, both in interpretation, application, preaching or teaching. No one was safe and no one deserved my self-righteous condemning wrath but that's what rogue assassins do.

My new innocent girlfriend back home was a casualty. (We eventually broke up) Then my parents took some hits. (I moved out) Then my pastor and the people in my home church tried to reel me in. (I resigned my membership)

Then I felt the necessity to go on search and destroy missions. I wrote letters, I made phone calls, I stopped by homes of my old friends from high school and first asked their forgiveness then confronted them at close range with scriptural kill shots. All in the name of 'saving' them from the life of sin that I knew they lived because I lived it with them.

I was a psychological and spiritual mess and now armed with the very Word of God. I was a real piece of work—I was young, puffed up with pride, brash, articulate, and disciplined. I was the perfect storm of vice, judgmental cynicism, limited authoritarian-based knowledge and righteous indignation—with a dash of charm and a pinch of flirty mischievousness.

I had fulfilled my wager with God and later that summer, sat out on that same dock on a moon lit night. I certainly had changed on the outside and gained tremendous knowledge of the Bible but I was still no closer to God—still empty. I raised my fist into the air and said, "One more year, God. One more year to prove this Christian life is worth living."

∞

Over the next year of my life I would change spiritual directions again because of a friendship with a pastor who asked me to stay on after my summer internship. He thought he could withstand my biblical assaults. I questioned his Christianity, his calling to be a pastor and even his salvation on a canoe ride that summer because he didn't hold to a literal six day creation interpretation of Genesis. I don't know why he didn't throw me from the canoe right then and there. But he didn't. Rather, he showed me a different way to be a Christian. He was a true friend and I have thanked God every day for him.

He unsettled me with questions. Was I sure God could fit in my little theological box? Which people in the New Testament used rule keeping as a spiritual measuring stick? Which character are you in Jesus's parables? He assured me God was not afraid of any question I might ask. So I started to ask questions with him. We both thought something needed to change about how Christianity was being lived out so we would set out on a quest for a real relationship with God.

The Christian life became more adventurous and loving. I still struggled greatly with sin, guilt, spiritual depression and doubt. As I shed the brainwashing of trying to perform for God's love and bring together the spiritual schizophrenia of my past I confessed to him that I still felt empty, off somehow or too damaged inside. He told me only God could fill that emptiness in my heart. I agreed with him but didn't really know what he meant. I wanted so badly to live an authentic Christian life. He warned me that it would be hard for me. I would have to unlearn the version of God I believed in. He told me it was okay to lay down my 'rifle' and to trust God to lead me to a more fulfilling life and greater understanding of who He really was.

With his help, I would start to unlearn God. I would also dull the edge in my personality because I saw people very different from me living out their spirituality, their Christian walk—liberal people that played cards! Was my year wasted at Word of Life? What about all that I had learned—was it wrong, misguided or were they right and the rest of history and Christendom wrong?

They say once a Marine, always a Marine—would that be true for me and my boot camp experience at WOLBI? It seemed that God was exposing me to extremes and it begged re-evaluation of everything. I started to question everything about my life, my version of Christianity and God. I only half listened to my pastor friend about laying down my rifle. It was my identity for so long and was more comfortable than the uncertainty of questioning everything, but my days as a biblical assassin were definitely numbered.

That fall I had lunch with a friend from my home church and fellow WOLBI student. He had stayed on for the second year at WOLBI. I listened to him and observed how he quoted the Bible. I shared with him where I was spiritually, questioning everything. Soon the language, trust and camaraderie crumbled. He started quoting the Bible at me. He was concerned for me. He tried to reel me back into the fold of the WOLBI version of true biblical Christianity.

For weeks after my lunch with my old WOLBI friend I had a type of spiritual post-traumatic stress syndrome. Was I making a mistake with my life? Should I go back to the Christianity of my youth? I knew that way. I was a superstar Christian there. When I was at WOLBI I had biblical answers for everything and now all I had were questions. I was day to day dealing with doubt, guilt and some severe spiritual head injuries.

I decided to press on with my pastor friend. I doubled down on my wager with God and gave Him two more years. I needed to figure some stuff out. I volunteered as an intern in the youth program at the mega church, taught, preached, listened to all kinds of music, read all kinds of books, played cards constantly. I was trying to heal myself by being busy in the ministry so I would stop sinning and punishing myself for past sins.

Being busy in ministry didn't work. I knew it but never talked about it because what else was a Christian supposed to do? I knew my Bible, I was in ministry but when I would slyly hold back that gay looking Jesus bower and slap a 'euchre' on someone in cards, I still felt a little guilty for a whole host of spiritually injured reasons.

r. leo olson

DIAGNOSING SPIRITUAL HEAD INJURIES

After graduating from WOLBI, I took a semester off and worked odd jobs in the clogs of retail sales. I was quickly pigeon-holed as a spiritual 'holier than thou' Bible thumper. I took some classes at several local colleges to keep my foot in the door of academia. I was living on my own, not dating, volunteering as an intern at a mega-church and on an exclusive diet of Mac-N-Cheese, Ramen noodles, and oatmeal cream pies. A special meal was either the youth group pizza parties or whatever Meijer Thrifty Acres was sampling on Saturday mornings. I was a drifting college kid amassing school debt and developing my now type 2-Diabetes because beggars can't be concerned about health food.

I needed to keep my school loans in deferment, so I enrolled full time at Grand Rapids Junior College. I wanted to finish some straggling core classes of my patch-worked educational transcript before I chose a college and declared a major and set the world on fire with my special kind of Christianity. My time was spent foraging for food at church gatherings, searching for a wife, repressing my raging hormones by reading the most condemning passages of the Bible about lust and trying not to be a spiritually odd person. I had little success in all areas.

I sat in the back of my first class at Grand Rapids Junior College as the rabble of newly graduated high schoolers stumbled into Spanish 101. The professor was late and there was absolutely no energy or glimmer of enthusiasm in the room. The woman next to me was Hispanic and older than me by ten years, easy, and I suspected she was a mother trying to finish her general-education requirements.

After some pleasant chit chat my suspicions were verified. I felt comfortable around her immediately. There was something about her—not sexual energy or a latent Freudian 'marry your mother' complex but something. I was drawn to her like no other woman I had met before.

"Don't you know Spanish already?" I asked.

She laughed and jibed me for being racist.

"I do know Spanish but I needed some easy credits to graduate with my associates and I have some really tough classes this semester—plus being a mom—it's hectic—what about you?"

"No, I don't speak Spanish, just trying to get some core classes under my belt and transfer."

"So what are you going to study?" she asked.

"Well, I have a degree in Bible right now, so probably something in a church, a pastor or Bible professor," I said.

"A Bible degree? What are you a Baptist?" she said and laughed.

I was caught off guard by her laughter. It was infectious, loud but not embarrassing.

"Yes I'm a Baptist, well raised one anyway, but, why is that so funny? What are you?"

"I'm Catholic. I'm sorry I wasn't really laughing at you."

"Yes, you were." I quipped back and smiled.

"Promise me you're not going to quote Scripture at me and try to save me all semester?"

I looked at her, smiled because she was smiling at me. Honestly, I did want to do just that—saving a Catholic was like big game hunting for Protestants. Here was my chance. I had her in the cross-hairs of my scope, ready to pull the trigger but said, "What? No, of course not. I mean I can if you want me too—but—well, sounds like you've met some Baptists before." (Misfire!)

"Oh yes, every Baptist I've met has quoted the Bible to me and tried to save me. You'd think by now they would have figured out we don't know our Bible like they do. We don't use the Bible in the same way either," she said and smiled a smile that melted all my biblical aggressive conversion instincts.

It was this last phrase that has stuck in my head over the years—'we don't use the Bible the same way you do." This woman, who I would never see again after Spanish 101, was the first person to help diagnose some my spiritual head injuries.

During the course we grew to be friends. Her inner joy was infectious. Her concerns, the problems that she would share with me about her life, had to do with others' sufferings—her child's cold, her grandmother's ailing body, her extended family in Mexico, her brother sowing 'wild oats' and ruining his life. She had a selflessness about her that was disgustingly authentic and I wanted it. She was a virtuous woman and I envied her virtue.

I asked questions about the Bible and Catholicism and how she lived out her faith. Her life did not match up with the nurtured animosity and stereotypes that I had been taught about the Catholics. She did not believe her works would save her yet she was consumed with doing good works for others. She did not sin and then run to the priest, say a "Hail Mary' to a little idol statue and then move on—she grieved for her sins and begged the Virgin Mary to help her love others like she loved her Son. She had a deep, strong and personal faith in God. She performed selfless works, prayed the rosary daily, loved others, felt repentance, transformation and had real joy but didn't read her Bible. How could this woman be a better Christian than me? I could 'chapter and verse' the mess out of her.

One time, I pressed her for why she didn't read her Bible more. "So you never read your Bible, why not? You know it's a good book?"

"It's not that I don't ever read the Bible. I do at Mass and at other times. It's just there's more to it than reading your Bible that makes someone a Christian—plus you Protestants read it wrong." She laughed again. She was sassy but nice about it.

"Wow, so I read my Bible wrong? Really?" I said and perked up. Those were fighting words.

"Yeah, it's hard to find a 'Bible thumping' Baptist who's not angry and telling people about their sins and hell...where's the love, brother?"

I was about to reach for my pistol; "God is a just judge,

and God is angry with the wicked every day" (Psalm 7:11). BANG! But she smiled, and winked at me this time, and totally disarmed me with love.

Class started and I let her have the last word in that conversation because, well, she was right and I knew it. I didn't want to believe her but how could I argue against a life marked with such love for others and the energy of the Holy Spirit? What was I going to convert her to or save her from? She had the life I had wagered with God for on that dock.

The first diagnosis of my spiritual head injuries: I have read my Bible wrong and was misusing it on others and myself.

∞

My Intro. to Lit. professor was a gay Christian man. He said it right in class. I freaked out inside because I wasn't sure gay people could be Christians. My spiritual head injuries produced some ridiculous inner dialogues at times. I grabbed my Bible out of my backpack at the first break and looked up a familiar underlined passage and read:

"Do you not know that the unrighteous will not inherit the kingdom of God? Do not be deceived. Neither fornicators, nor idolaters, nor adulterers, nor homosexuals, nor sodomites, nor thieves, nor covetous, nor drunkards, nor revilers, nor extortioners will inherit the kingdom of God" (I Corinthians 6:9-10).

That seemed pretty clear cut but did I understand it right? Was I misusing it? I wasn't sure I could be excused from that list. I decided to reserve judgment because I wasn't at a

Christian college so rubbing shoulders with worldly people was to be expected. I holstered my Bible and did not drop the class but resolved I would never shake his hand or visit him alone during office hours.

He was older, educated, a true professional and went to an Episcopalian church—of course, the Episcopalians take everyone I thought. He was a guest professor and had taught literature for many years at various colleges.

I smirked at the reading list from the syllabus. There were several books by openly gay authors. I was taught to 'hate the sin and love the sinner,' and hate especially the gay sins. I grew up finding it easier to forgive Judas Iscariot than a gay person. Homosexuality was the most abhorrent sin anyone could commit; next to pedophilia, but that was lumped in with gay sex anyway.

In truth, I could not separate the sin from the sinner. I was disgusted with how gay men talked and dressed. I was grossed out with lesbians who did not shave their legs. I found the whole gay culture repulsive but my hatred had nothing to do with the actual sexual acts they did—I never really thought about the sex acts except in crude Christian jokes. I hated the sin and the sinner. Once again I found myself on the other side of love holding my Bible against everyone's head like a gun.

I enjoyed the class and the discussions he lead. He was a man that was open-minded but not in the way that he would say 'anything goes'. He had convictions and beliefs but listened, really listened, and tried to understand where the student was coming from. He was the first openly gay man I had spent any time with and I learned a lot from him about literature and life, not just gay literature. I was not threatened by him in any way but kept my hand on my homophobic holster, just in case I needed it.

I didn't magically become gay or talk with a lisp from being in his presence. I came to admire him.[18] He was a good man, a great professor and I had come to believe he was a Christian. Especially when we read James Baldwin's *Giovanni's Room* and had the most poignant class discussion about being gay and a Christian.

There were other Christians who were raised like me in the class, but no one with real biblical assassin training. They voiced their objections in the discussion with sound bite theological statements and Bible verses they had heard from their pastors but with no real conviction, just general condemnation. Counter arguments arose from people who were not particularly religious, just the average laissez-faire social liberals. And there were people who just waited the whole thing out because it was a necessary three credit class that fulfilled the English requirement. I ended up being one of the silent ones. I wanted to jump in, get off a couple rounds and hunker down in a fox hole again, but didn't.

The professor was tolerant of all views and a fair moderator because what was happening in the class discussion was

---

[18] 15 years later I ran into him at a bookstore and reminisced about my time in his class. He encouraged me to continue to write and publish even if I never sell more than fifty books—"Literature tells the stories of our lives for future generations." This conversation was one of my divine promptings for writing this memoir as I referenced in the Author's Note.

one of the main themes in <u>Giovanni's Room</u>—the struggle a gay person experiences by being treated as a second class human being in society because of being gay.

As the professor closed the discussion the Christians grew more adamant and angry, and it was obvious the social libs were just trying to piss them off. It was like the Cuban Missile Crisis—the ominous stress of potential spiritual nuclear war but no causalities.

In his closing statement he said, "God made me and you and James Baldwin and all of us. God loves you and God loves me—this I know for the Bible tells me so," he sang out.

Everyone laughed and tensions lessoned.

"God commands us to love one another in spite of all our sins. Baldwin's book is asking where in society is it okay to go and be loved as a human being. Gay or not, we are all created by God, and dealing with all kinds of pain about not fitting in, not being loved. Baldwin's writings are about social divisions and their destructiveness—about how labels dehumanize people. Did you listen to the discussion we just had? It illustrated the tension and controversy of Giovanni's Room perfectly. Where can a gay person find love in America? The church?—among the Christians?—is that a safe place for a gay man to receive God's love? If not there and with loving Christians, then where are humans supposed to hear and experience God's unconditional love?" the professor said then smiled.

There was a long pause, like when a preacher waits for someone to come down front during an altar call. No one said a word. It was a question we all had to deal with in our hearts and I was out of ammo.

"Let's leave *Giovanni's Room* and move on to *The Heart of Darkness* by Joseph Conrad—maybe he can enlighten us."

I thought my professor's questions were valid. Does God love only parts of us? Does He only love us when we do the right things or act certain ways? Did He withhold his love when I had acted like a horny drunkard but not when I won preaching contests? There was deep theology in conflict in my Lit class—too deep for me to resolve but I walked away with a couple of concrete thoughts.

God was God and God had worked out how He can be love and hate sin and not be two Gods. I could not do this. I could not 'hate the sin and love the sinner' without setting myself up as a judge, wielding an arsenal of brutal and eternal condemnation shots from my rifle. I wanted to love God and 'my neighbor' the same way God loved them, but since I could not resolve the paradox of loving and hating anything at the same time; I decided I needed to learn how to error on the side of trying to love others without judgment.

The second diagnosis of my spiritual head injuries: Withhold all judgments; listen to know the best way to love all people because we are all sinners. We all fight a thousand battles in life. Who was I to wage war on someone God dearly loved?

∞

Every Monday, Wednesday and Friday, I walked into the main building of the junior college. No matter what time of day it was; rain, snow, or shine a huddle of what I called 'beat nicks' would waft cigarette smoke and sip sugary caffeine mixtures in the doorway. I usually held my breath and hustled through the door.

There were also flyers posted over the doors and entry walls. They were politically slanted left and had to do with civil rights being violated or the evils of 'big business' exploiting the common man. And many scientific looking flyers claiming the benefits of marijuana and a call to action that it should be legalized.

One day a young white man with dread-locks handed me a post-card sized Reggae fundraiser notice for marijuana legalization. He was quite an active person on the campus and I always kept my eye out for him—white men with dreads are unforgettable and always interesting people.

Later that week, in between classes, I noticed that Dread-lock was in a passionate discussion with some 'Bible thumpers' about how Democrats are not true Christians. They argued that what was wrong with America was that liberals were trying to get government to do the work of the Church through socialistic programs. The problems of the world would go away if everyone lived a Christian life. Getting people saved was the 'Great Commission'[19] not big government. My ears were perked and anticipated a biblical blood

---

[19] "And Jesus came and spoke to them, saying, 'All authority has been given to Me in heaven and on earth. Go therefore and make disciples of all the nations, baptizing them in the name of the Father and of the Son and of the Holy Spirit, teaching them to observe all things that I have commanded you; and lo, I am with you always, *even* to the end of the age.' Amen" (Matthew 28:18-20). This passage is commonly called the Great Commission that Jesus gave to His disciples.

bath, so I sat close to eves-drop on the debate.

The biblical assassin squad ganged up on him all cross firing him with their shots. Dread-lock held his own. I was surprised and started to root for him—*I love an underdog*. He claimed to be a 'Believer in Jesus' but accused them of being 'born-again' right wing bigots and Christian fascists.

"I live out the teachings of Jesus and leave the theology to people on the side-lines," was his final blow.

The biblical hand grenades of quoting verses yielded to a standstill—it was time to go back and reload and some had to get to class. Dread-lock sat down and opened his text book one table over from me.

"That was quite an exchange," I said.

"Yeah, I don't get why they can't see Jesus loved every-one, no matter what and cared about social justice issues, I mean, live it out, right? Church is a verb, man," he said.

I liked Dread-lock and remembered that "Faith without works is dead" (James 2:20). He was the first of the liberal Democrat beatniks I would meet. After witnessing that exchange I decided to breath in their second hand smoke and try and learn the ways of the beatniks—their thinking, their moral compass and more admirably their application of the Bible in the realms of political and social justice.

I also intentionally did not quote the Bible in conversations after being embarrassed by the 'hit squad'. I wasn't embar-rassed about being a Christian but about how my version of Christianity treated the so called 'lost', the dread-locked, marijuana smoking beatniks, and the Democrats of the social left.

The third diagnosis of my spiritual head injuries: Get my Christianity out of my own head and get off the sidelines.

∞

At the junior college, I met my first Catholic mom, gay guy, and liberal Democrat beatnik. The surprising thing about those three very different people was I liked each of them very much and I did not become a Catholic, gay, or a liberal Democrat beatnik, like I had been fear mongered into believing by my upbringing and training. The unsettling thing was that those three were all better Christians than I was. I wasn't sure what the hell was going on with me and God and Christianity.

It was at junior college that I realized my version of Christianity was deformed in my head. It was a weird kind of spiritual masturbation of inner arguments about my beliefs that isolated me from other believers. I really was standing 'alone on the Word of God' and the theology of that little song was the only assurance of me being a Christian.

I was cultish in the way I interacted with society, politics and the arts. I was spiritually inbred with others in what I called good Christian fellowship, although the more I talked theology with them the more I disagreed with everyone. My Christian mission was not to love my brother whether Catholic, liberal, gay. It was to save, convert, recruit, and defend my version of biblical Christianity by faulty argumentation, prideful condemnation and biblical assassinations. I felt ignorant, deceived, purposely not getting the whole picture, even tricked by my Christian upbringing. I was mean. I was scared, confused and was riddled with doubt about God, the Bible, and every version of my spiritually schizophrenic self.

∞

After junior college I spent the rest of my college days commuting to Cornerstone University, still volunteering at the mega-church and living alone trying to think my way out of these spiritual head injuries. I learned of psychology, sociology, history, world religions and many other things that were often demonized in the 'Bible is the only source of truth' worldview I was raised with—it was much less so at Cornerstone but it was a safe place to sort through some of my issues. I studied literature in-depth and was taken with Hemingway especially his short stories—*Hills Like White Elephants* was my second favorite, his use of emotionally packed dialogue hooked me but *Today is Friday* [20] blew my mind. *The Hound of Heaven* by Francis Thompson mesmerized me. I especially appreciated the older English because it reminded me of my KJV, which I'd stopped reading. The poem spoke of a different way in which God worked than I knew—not angry, chasing me down to confront me about my sins but pursuing me. I wondered if God was hunting me down.

It was in my closing years of college that I began to understand my philosophy classes and took more of them. A mental

---

[20] A short story about the conversations three Roman soldiers had over beers at a pub after crucifying Jesus.

revolution happened when I finally put together that all people understand the world, God, and reality with foundational 'presuppositions'. Everyone has these foundational presuppositions. They are necessary for human knowledge and even something so common as language. The real revelation for me was that some of my presuppositions were faulty, especially when it came to the role and interpretation of the Bible.[21]

My Catholic mom friend was right. I was reading my Bible wrong. I didn't like the 'presuppositions' I held about the Christian life, God, the Bible, and my mission in it. They were too small minded and did not produce the life of virtue and love I saw in others. Many of which I judged as lost, hell-bound, and 'non-Christian'.

Of course the problem was within my own head again and it was in my last semester of college that I saw the severity of my spiritual head injuries. I realized I had become a prideful, combative, self-absorbed, insecure Christian ass. I was spiritually depressed and wanted to chuck the whole thing. Thank God I found the writings of Soren Kierkegaard, Rudolph Otto and, Fr. Henri Nouwen. I also listened to the Christian contemporary music of Michael Card, Charlie Peacock and Keith Green to break up the quiet moments of total spiritual despair.

My 'wagerous' ways had given out to a long term recovery plan for my spiritual head injuries. I could no longer trust my

---

[21] In this context I mean the act of presuming things to be true about a subject before gaining knowledge about the subject and thus creating contradictory or faulty arguments to defend the presupposition

own thoughts about God, life or Christianity.

I was having an existential 'Garden of Gethsemane' trial. [22] I was frightened to unlearn God. It was unsettling to the very core of my being to question and reevaluate the role of the Bible—my only trusted source of knowledge about God. It was like cutting the anchor rope and drifting out into an ocean of spiritual uncertainty. I didn't want to second guess all those who had raised me in a Christian faith tradition and think that they could have been well intentioned but off the mark.

Honestly I was terrified that I would become too liberal or get sent to hell or worse give up and win my wager with God that the Christian life was not worth living. I mean, it's one thing to raise a fist to God on a dock, but to step out into the darkness in faith, hoping God will meet you there, trusting Him, that is some frightening existential shit.

But what could I do? I still had this inexpressible hunger for an authentic expression of the Christian life, for God, for something real but I didn't know where to look any more. I started to read the wisdom literature of the Bible more. I underlined Ecclesiastes 3:11, "He has made everything beautiful in its time. Also He has put eternity in their hearts, except that no one can find out the work that God does from beginning to end." *Great*.

---

[22] "Then Jesus went with his disciples to a place called Gethsemane, and he said to them, 'Sit here while I go over there and pray.' He took Peter and the two sons of Zebedee along with him, and he began to be sorrowful and troubled. Then he said to them, 'My soul is overwhelmed with sorrow to the point of death. Stay here and keep watch with me...'" (Matthew 26:36-46).

I wanted to wager with God again as I closed out my college studies but gambling was prohibited by the college code of conduct. So I continued to stand at the cliff's edge of Christianity as I knew it and hoped that God would catch me if I took my leap into the dark.

SPIRITUAL HUNGER CRAMPS

I was delivering flowers for a floral company, one of my many college jobs. It was definitely my favorite job because every delivery ended in someone smiling. It was nice to see smiles when I was spiritually depressed and riddled with seemingly paradoxical questions about an all-powerful, beneficent, loving God giving me the enormous responsibility of trying to save people from the burning fires of hell. I professed salvation from a Savior that God the Father killed and had exacted payment on a bloody cross for all our sins and offered a cultish separation from the evil world as the Christian life based on an inerrant, literal interpretation of the Bible. Christian doctrine started to sound like propaganda cheers from opposing high school cheer leaders, 'we got spirit yes we do, we got spirit how about you?' Only it was the six-literal days of creation Baptists versus the Howard Van Till's Theistic Evolution reformed theology theories.[23]

There were endless major and minor theological/biblical debates like this in Protestant higher education that I was

---

[23] In 1988 Howard Van Till a professor at Calvin College co-wrote *Science Held Hostage: What's wrong with creation science and evolution.* It was much debated theory over the interpretation of Genesis and yet another doctrinal point to divide Protestant Christians.

supposed to somehow pick the winning side and defend the position through out of context Bible verses and red herring logical sound bites. I had witnessed the interpretive 'spin' in higher level biblical criticism and the translation free-for-all in Greek classes. But I was too injured to discern anything anymore, let alone biblical truth being debated by much smarter scholars.

All together now, The B-I-B-L-E, yes that's the book for me, I stand alone on the word of God, the B-I-B-L-E, Bible! It was becoming a tough sell.

I also had crushing self-abasing guilt haunting my sinful memories no matter how many verses I memorized about God's forgiveness. I was not worthy nor equipped to lead people in any type of Christian way of life. Hell, I was having a hard time finding my own way. How could I recruit others to this problematic view of God being pissed off at our sins and yet speak of the inner joyous life of a Christian in some future ministry? I was told I was given a gift of preaching by the Holy Spirit. I was told I was special in God's eyes, even more special than others because of my obvious gifts acknowledged by winning contests. I was a two time national champion preacher boy after all. It was time to decide if I would go to seminary or not after graduation.

It would have been so much easier to stop questioning the Bible, stop wagering with God and just put on the Sunday suit and go with the flow but I couldn't. This inner spiritual 'angst' was killing me and it made delivering flowers a much more wonderful thing to do with my time than thinking about being a pastor or Bible college professor.

∞

One particular 'run' as it's called in the flower delivery biz took me way out into the countryside down a long road called Parnell. At the end of Parnell Road nestled among the gentle rolling pastures sat St. Patrick's Catholic Church.

As a young Baptist boy, I was taught Catholics were trying to 'work for their salvation' and in danger of hell for misunderstanding the biblical plan of salvation. Well, maybe not all Catholics, there was that one Catholic mom in Spanish 101, but the ones that believed their works would get them to heaven were in sure danger. Just look at their church buildings—idolatrous hangouts with statues of Mary, magic wafers and holy water fonts that were only good for fighting demons in movies.

I had been to this Catholic Church once before, about a year earlier with my Religion in America class. We had visited many different places of worship and St. Patrick's was the Catholic Church closest to my professor's house. We sat through a Saturday evening Mass and I had a bunker bomb of a verse marked out in my Bible for every liturgical act of idolatry I had witnessed that evening: "You shall not make idols for yourselves; neither a carved image nor a sacred pillar shall you rear up for yourselves; nor shall you set up an engraved stone in your land, to bow down to it; for I am the Lord your God" (Leviticus 26:1). *Ka-Boom!*

When the Q & A part of the class trip into the *synagogue of Satan* happened, like a sniper, I waited until the end to ask my 'kill shot' question. The priest was a portly man with a struggling beard, red cheeks and thinning hair, like a young Santa Claus. He was so gracious as my classmates asked all kinds of questions, being the first time most of them had been in a Catholic Church.

"Pastor? *I call no man father.*[24] I have one last question; are you saved?" I asked. This was the only question that mattered to me.

He looked at me, hands folded over his roundness and smiled at me. I smirked back. I can still hear the tone in his voice as he answered, "Young man, I sure hope so, I've given my life to Him."

It wasn't the answer that caught me off guard; to me it was a yes or no question and he answered it wrong. It was his sincerity of really giving his life to God with no doubts or plan b's or wagers that shunned me into silence with no follow-up biblical versed assault.

He was a celibate priest and to a horny college student there was no greater sacrifice to God than sexual abstinence. He walked his talk and I backed down. We ended our visit but to this day his answer and the look in his eyes—no his soul, has stuck with me. He had something that I did not and that memory compelled me to stop in a year later at St. Patrick's after I dropped off my last flower delivery. I was looking for another sign from God.

The church was open but no one was present. I stepped in further and looked around. I checked the holy water dish for

---

[24] "Do not call anyone on earth your father; for One is your Father, He who is in heaven" (Matthew 23:9).

water and rubbed my fingers dry on my jeans. I took a seat in the back pew and looked at all the statues. I wanted to hear the floor to ceiling pipe organ. It smelled different than Protestant churches. But I wasn't drawn to the Italian flavored pictures of Christ, invisible winds blowing His robes and thorns *around* his bleeding and glowing heart. He _wore_ a crown of thorns on his head, was my first thought but I kept my biblical handgun holstered. I thumbed through the missal and wondered. I prayed to God to show me a sign. He did not so I stopped praying. I looked at the angels and wondered some more in silence. I could feel something there but I had been so severely injured thinking that Catholicism was the road to hell that I remained suspicious.

I knew something was wrong with how I had put my Christianity together. I believed all the right things but I felt like I was never living up to God's expectations with my version of Christianity. Maybe I should join the Catholics and be like that sincere priest or my friend from Spanish 101. I liked Pope John Paul II, he seemed like a holy guy. Was that my 'sign'—that in my darkest hours of inner spiritual turmoil I randomly stop into a Catholic Church looking for God?

Maybe I wasn't really saved? No, it couldn't have been that. I had assured myself that the formula for salvation had been transacted in my life many times—hundreds of times. I reminded myself that I was baptized twice, once after the 'hell movie' as a boy with the headless motorcycle rider and again at WOLBI. If there were any doubts because of my 'wild oat sowing' ways I had 'rededicated' myself to the Lord with tears on my pillow and with all night Bible reading countless times.

I had everything in its right category and I was too biblically knowledgeable to have such a crisis of faith now—but I was. I was about to graduate from a Baptist college and go to its adjoining seminary and yet I knew I was missing something. Now this ol' Baptist preacher boy was sitting in a Catholic Church—*Houston we have a problem.*

My heart longed for more but I was too scared to venture out of my upbringing, out from the Protestant tradition promising me a good and comfortable life. I was fearful that I would become an Amplified Bible reading, woman pastor supporting liberal Christian at best and a Catholic at worst. I was fearful that I might get tricked by the demons into some new age mystical experience if I believed in angels or miracles or anything resembling mystical Christianity. I was fearful that I would not have a ministry or a career if I did not tow the Baptist line. I was fearful that the 'rapture' would happen before I had a chance to have guilt free marital sex.

What I yearned for was a life filled with divine intervention like Abraham, Joshua or the Apostles. I wanted to see a vision like Isaiah, Ezekiel, Paul or John. I wanted to experience God in some real way not just listening to good sermons or having a warm fuzzy feeling while reading gold leafed thin pages.

At this point, I would have even taken a highly suspect supernatural or mystical experience like I had heard about in fringe Catholicism. I wanted the physicality that I saw in Catholicism and the quiet mysticism of the sacraments and definitely the power over demons that holy water and other Catholic holy tools could give me. But all I had was the Bible, my doctrinal statements and codes of conduct to make up my spiritual soup of Christianity.

I wanted God to be bigger than what I had been raised to believe. I had spiritual hunger cramps. I had nagging questions that haunted my prayers. I was paralyzed with guilt from my sins and fear of God coming back when I was committing those sins. What if God came back when I was at the movies, violating the college code of conduct? What kind of testimony was that? What if God came back when I was making out with a girl trying to unhook a bra with one hand? What kind of testimony was that? Why was I not experiencing 'the way, the truth, and the life' Jesus promised?[25] Maybe I was? I went to church all the time, I knew the Bible very well and I believed all the right things, but so what?

I sat in that back pew for twenty minutes wondering if I had the guts to take a leap of faith and question everything in a quest to find God or life or whatever I was missing. Did I have it in me to make more wagers with God?

Jesus tells a story that all the angels in heaven rejoice over one sinner that repents.[26] He likened it to a poor woman who had ten coins and lost one. She turned her house upside down to find the one coin and then told all her friends what she had found.[27]

---

[25] "Jesus said to him, 'I am the way, the truth, and the life. No one comes to the Father except through Me'" (John 14:6).

[26] "I say to you that likewise there will be more joy in heaven over one sinner who repents than over ninety-nine just persons who need no repentance" (Luke 15:17).

[27] "Or what woman, having ten silver coins, if she loses one coin, does not light a lamp, sweep the house, and search carefully until she finds *it?* And

I decided that day to make another wager with God in a Catholic Church of all places. I needed to find what I was missing, no matter where it took me. I stood up from the pew and walked up to the holy water dish and dipped my fingers in it. I wiped a cross on my forehead, hoping it would kick-start the healing process of my spiritual head injuries, and was ready to turn my spiritual house upside down. I needed more than the Bible and codes of conduct and endless doctrinal statement debates. I needed more than what I had built up in my own mind as Christianity. If the Hound of heaven was hunting for me, He'd better hurry up because I was on the verge of spiritual insanity. This was an all or nothing wager.

∞

Before graduation from college I felt more alone with less and less people to talk with, to question with, to sojourn with. I thought maybe if I moved away I could find other confused and spiritually injured souls or a bigger spectrum of conservative-liberal Christians that could help me.

It had been a couple of months since I bellied up to the roulette table and wagered with God at that Catholic Church and He had been pretty quiet since then. So, I applied to several different seminaries in Chicago, New York and California, where all the liberal Christians were. I made a side bet with God that I would go somewhere else unless He made

when she has found *it*, she calls *her* friends and neighbors together, saying, 'Rejoice with me, for I have found the piece which I lost!' Likewise, I say to you, there is joy in the presence of the angels of God over one sinner who repents" (Luke 15:7-10).

it clear that I should stay here—crystal clear, same rules as before.

I still wanted to date because the pool of good looking Christian women significantly drops when you graduate. It's just the fact of the matter—a numbers game. Since I had a backup plan for a new life, somewhere else, I decided to be brave and ask out the prettiest girl I knew.

Emily walked up to me at the end of a Wednesday night youth group meeting and casually asked what I had been up to lately.

"Go out for coffee with me and I'll tell you." Not a particularly smooth line but effective. She laughed. I can still see the smile and the slight tilt of her head as she looked at me, not knowing if this was an actual 'asking out'. She tried to inquire again and I repeated the line. It worked.

On October 11th nineteen ninety-four, I had my first date with Emily at Javasphere, a local coffee shop. We saw each other every day until January 11th nineteen ninety-five when I asked her to marry me.

I promised her a life of financial poverty, years of spiritual instability, a slim hope of a meaningful career in a really liberal church or Christian college, my whole heart and injured soul. I don't know what she heard me say but she said, 'yes'. May 19th nineteen ninety-five we were married, seven months after our first date. We had a quick courtship to the utter surprise of our parents, but when you know, you know. Why wait?

I wish I could say life with Emily fixed all my spiritual head injuries. I wish I could say my love for her quenched my spiritual hunger cramps and happy marital bliss now filled my waking moments. But no person can do that totally for another and happiness is never the goal of a marriage; only a blessed by-product of a good one. However, Emily loved me, the real, injured, broken me and she has been a constant example of true, real, divine love for me ever since that first sip of coffee.

God had acted pretty clearly again and I had to pony up to my side of the bargain. I was glad to stay in Grand Rapids and attend Grand Rapids Baptist Seminary as long as it was with Emily. Coffee truly is the nectar of the gods.

PROTESTANT PURGATORY

I died at seminary. The exact moment was in a systematic theology class and the discussion was about hermeneutics[28] and the professor used Kierkegaard's[29] critiques of cultural Christianity to prove a point. It was a lively lecture by a very pious and humble man. He brought up a point in the academic discussion and cautioned us about interpreting the Bible as a literal objective truth source without accounting for flawed reasoning and subjective interpretations in the human conscience and even broader cultural subjectivities.

My jaw dropped open and I looked around the room at my fellow students—*glassy eyed lemmings*. I was still an arrogant Christian ass. I leaned over to a friend and said, "Did you just hear that? He quoted Kierkegaard to prove his point."

"Everybody quotes Kant and Kierkegaard but who really understands those guys anyway," was his response.

It was a fair response because Kierkegaard's writings are pretty thick—slow thoughtful reading for sure. But if what the professor said held any truth, then we all could have

---

[28] Biblical hermeneutics is the science that teaches the principles and methods of interpreting the Bible

[29] 1813-1855; Soren Kierkegaard was a Danish philosopher, theologian and religious author. He is widely considered to be the first Christian existentialist philosopher.

'flawed reason' and be mentally shackled with subjective sinfully biased consciences that I was told was the voice of the Holy Spirit when interpreting the Bible. The same Bible that we held as an inerrant, literal, objective truth source and the final authority for life and faith according to the seminary's doctrinal statement. For me, that was a fatal blow to Luther's foundational strand of the Protestant Reformation.[30]

I walked up to the professor during the break and clarified my concerns about what he said during the lecture.

"It's a real issue to consider," he said.

During the second hour of his lecture, he referenced our little conversation during the break and left the issue of biblical interpretation in tension for us young preacher boys to wrestle with.

My Greek and Hebrew classes dealt me just as damaging death blows. Any honest historical-critical evaluation of biblical translation will reveal a number of issues that conflict with cornerstone Protestant beliefs concerning what the Bible is, compared to what it is presented or claimed to be in Protestant preaching and doctrinal statements. For example there is no way Isaiah was written by one person—the Hebrew is so different; like claiming Shakespeare knew

---

[30] "Unless I am convinced by the testimony of the Scriptures or by clear reason (for I do not trust either in the pope or in councils alone, since it is well known that they have often erred and contradicted themselves), **I am bound by the Scriptures I have quoted and my conscience is captive to the Word of God.** I cannot and will not recant anything, since it is neither safe nor right to go against conscience. May God help me. Amen." Luther's Response to the Inquisition at the Diet of Worms 1521.

Ebonics. The book of Daniel is a mess. On and on these conflicts started to mount the more I learned about translating.

Translating is not a word for word, tit for tat process. I learned that words represent concepts that are culturally nuanced. The translator must make decisions about what the word meant in the ancient culture or a best guess. I heard many times, 'there is not an exact word for that in English' so we have to provide a 'dynamic equivalent'.

For example, Acts chapter 13 verse 2 reads: (New King James version)

> "As they **ministered** to the Lord and fasted, the Holy Spirit said, "Now separate to Me Barnabas and Saul for the work to which I have called them." (v3)Then, having fasted and prayed, and laid hands on them, they sent *them* away."

At first read it was no big deal except for the word **ministered**. I would sit with my New American Standard-Greek parallel translation and actually re-translate verses of the Bible: (Acts 13:2 in Greek with the English exact case-gender-tense word—tit for tat translation)

> **Λειτουργο**ύ**ντων** δὲ αὐτῶν τῷ κυρίῳ καὶ νηστευόντων εἶπεν τὸ πνεῦμα τὸ ἅγιον Ἀφορίσατε δή μοι τὸν Βαρνάβαν καὶ Σαῦλον εἰς τὸ ἔργον ὃ προσκέκλημαι αὐτούς.

Of-public-working-unto moreover of-them unto-the-one unto-Authority-belonged and of-non-eating-of it-had-said, the-one a-currenting-to the-one hallow-belonged, Ye-should-have-bounded-off-to then unto-me to-the-one to-a-Barnabas and to-a-Saulos into to-the-one to-a-work to-which I-had-come-to-call-toward-unto to-them.

What?

The Apostles were 'ministering' or 'Of-public-working' but what were they actually doing? This word **ministered**-**leitourgeo** {**li-toorg-eh'-o**} brought up certain mental pictures in my modern Protestant mind of how the early Apostles were **ministering and fasting** as they sent out Saul and Barnabas on a missionary journey—they sat around, sang songs with a lute or some guitar-type instrument, prayed and read the Old Testament Psalms. That's what my best guess of what early church worship or 'ministering' was.

However, I was reading some really interesting Catholic writers and Church Fathers from the Eastern Orthodox Church, too. I read that the Eastern Orthodox and Catholics fasted before their worship services called, **Liturgies**.

So "As they **Liturgized** to the Lord and fasted, the Holy Spirit said..." would be a valid translation of that exact phrase. But this word, 'Liturgy', brought up very different mental pictures—priests, chanting, vestments, Temple stuff, statues, icons, holy water and more formal religious rites, rubrics and traditions. I began to ask myself; what exactly were those apostles doing?

One problem with translating Scripture is that translators, or even the average reader, put their own 'traditions' and Christian presuppositions into the text and come up with different, conflicting 'dynamic equivalent' interpretations for the text. A translator can't help it. This is why an Eastern Orthodox, Catholic, Episcopalian, Lutheran, Calvinist, Baptist, Pentecostal, or however far you want to go down the schismatic family tree of the Christian church can read the same verse and have conflicting debates about the Bible and what it means.

Another example was in the 'Lord's prayer' or the 'Our Father'. Most Christians will pray this prayer with anyone. Like many things I was learning in seminary it provided a pseudo unifying effect as long as no one asked what it really meant.

All together now: Our Father who art in heaven, hallowed be thy name, thy kingdom come, they will be done on earth as it is in heaven. Give us this day our **daily** bread...[31]

This adjective '**daily**' in Greek is the word *Epiousios*. It's a hapax legomenon or a word that cannot be found anywhere in recorded classical Greek. No one actually knows what it means. It is not used anywhere else in writing to compare it to or get clues about its cultural context. This is a translator's nightmare.

The disciples asked Jesus Christ, the Son of God, the Messiah, the Promised One, how to pray and He used a word that

---

[31] The full prayer can be found in Matthew 6 and Luke 11.

Matthew and Luke certainly must have known what it meant because there were no clarifying follow-up questions, explanations, parables or anything recorded by the Gospel writers. They knew what the word *epiousios* meant but we don't.

I had heard many Protestant pastors preach that this word, *epiosios*, meant 'daily' because Jesus was trying to relate to the fishermen the idea of depending on God the Father for daily sustenance, a corollary phrase to 'God's will is done on earth as it is in heaven'. So a common dependence on God for daily needs as we prepare for a heavenly homecoming was the interpretative spin. It was only a reference to food or physical needs to make it through this life.

People pray this prayer all the time at dinner and even over fast food hoping God will bless it and make it healthy. I even preached this essential teaching of the Lord on prayer to teens at a youth group. It made sense and preached well within a Christian tradition that did not believe in sacraments but symbols.

But I wondered why use a word, an adjective so uncommon? It gnawed at me and I thought it would be interesting to do a typological search of the different kinds of *special breads* in the Old Testament. One example a Jewish believer would have surely correlated is the heavenly bread, manna, that God provided to the Israelites for forty years in the desert. Another special bread was the Shew-bread placed on a table in the Temple—a bread that was in the presence of Yahweh. It was also called the *bread of the presence*. This started to sound familiar to what the sacramental Catholics taught.

Then in the Gospels Jesus is doing some interesting things with bread. Certainly the disciples would have remembered Jesus's discourse recorded in John 6 where He says that His flesh is real food and you must eat it to be His disciples. Or the feeding of the five thousand and His claim to fame that He *was* the Bread of life. Or the last supper where He takes the bread and breaks it and says eat this in remembrance of Me. Or on the road to Emmaus when Luke, probably one of the guys eating with post-resurrected Jesus, wrote that, "...[Jesus] He was known to them *in* the breaking of bread" (Luke 24:35).

The 'daily' bread in the Lord's prayer was anything but common provisional bread. The *epiousios* was Jesus Himself. It was a super-celestial bread. It must have a physical reality and yet it hinted at a cosmically divine futuristic reality or meal or banquet. It was a mystical mysterious bread. It was a life giving bread not to fill your hungry gut but to give you a piece of divine life. The kind of bread that Jesus was talking about and the Gospel writers wrote about decades after His resurrection and decades with the Holy Spirit guiding them in all truth, was the Eucharistic bread—communion bread.[32]

Jesus was recorded by the Gospel writers to use a word, a heavenly conceptual adjective to describe what kind of bread we are to ask God for in prayer. It was more than a common loaf of bread—yeast, flour, water, salt; or to simply remind us to pray before meals or ask God for our physical *daily* bread

---

[32] Eucharist is a Greek word that means 'thanksgiving'. It is synonymous with Communion in Protestantism.

or *needs* as was commonly preached.

But I learned that a translator is always conditioned by the faith tradition he is in. My Greek professor used to ask us, 'does a fish know it's wet?' I laughed along-side all of my fellow students but didn't really understand the joke until my Protestant faith tradition, my water, would only allow me to translate a heavenly sacramental word as a common symbol. I knew I was wet and trapped in some dead water pond choking on doctrinal and theological restrictions dictating how to translate and interpret the Bible.

As I did this personally every day with the Scriptures I knew something was not right about how I was reading and now translating the meaning of God's words with my own feeble and inexperienced mind. I had clues about early church worship and now a sacramental worldview but no clear directions or signs from God.

Is this what seminarians and preachers really do? I was making shit up depending on which historical lens I was using. I would put on my ancient tradition lens to find verses to bash the Catholics for misinterpretations of the Bible or I would try to find new modern culturally relevant nuances for anecdotal sermon illustrations.

Greek manuscripts also differed from each other. Translating was very messy, confusing, and much like trying to steer a rudderless ship. *Whoa, hold the boat!*

I recognized the Bible held power over people and preachers had to interpret it in a certain way to uphold the

Protestant Reformation's cry of Sola Scriptura.[33] Somebody had to be in charge of this reformation, right? Was I going to be able to lead people with all my doubts? I started to ask more questions and read more broadly than the popularly approved commentaries. I wanted to know just how to use and interpret the authoritative Word of God properly. How did smarter men than me do it in the past? How did Paul instruct Timothy, a young 'seminarian' of sorts in the Bible?

I was shocked at a discovery while reading Paul's letters to Timothy. The 'Church' (an organically living, historically verifiable, organized and institutionalized body of believers at the time when this verse was penned) of the living God was 'the pillar and ground of truth'.[34] Apparently the New Testament was written to defend an already existent set of teachings about salvation, worship and the Christian life (Tradition) against a hostile world. The early church didn't have a Bible to quote at people to prove them wrong or lost or back-slidden. It was not preserved, copied, assembled over three hundred years to be mined by scholars or seminarians to provide ever new teachings or interpretations.

The Bible was used for instruction and as a type of liturgical book or guide for worship. It was a written witness to a

---

[33] The doctrine that the Bible only contains all knowledge necessary for salvation and holiness. Consequently, sola scriptura demands only doctrines that are found directly within or indirectly by using valid logical deduction or valid deductive reasoning from Scripture are spiritually authoritative.

[34] "I write so that you may know how you ought to conduct yourself in the house of God, which is the church of the living God, the pillar and ground of the truth" (I Timothy 3:15).

living divine-human cooperative—a history about God and a worshipping people. The chronicles, stories, letters and poetry that make up the Bible, especially the New Testament, were true and authoritative recorded witnesses to the people of God and how they were the historically verifiable, apostolically established and the one and only real living Church of God.

To divorce it from the historical community and reinterpret and really reinvent a different version of Christianity asks too much of the documents and necessarily puts too much trust in the subjectivity of the individual—on me a spiritually injured, naive seminarian hoping to earn a living in ministry. Is that what I was doing? Making up a hip modern personalized version of Christianity?

∞

Before graduation I was required to create my personal doctrinal statement. It was a litmus test to see if I was 'Baptist preacher' material. My future career hinged on it. I needed to play this role and provide for my family's future. Surly I was not the first guy to have these questions in seminary, I thought. But I did lack the courage to find the answers. So I detailed a personal doctrinal statement that would make me marketable to a number of congregations.

I detailed the best metaphors describing the Trinity from Augustine to Aquinas. I held the paradox of the divinity and humanity of Christ in equal balance according to the Seven

Ecumenical Councils.[35] Although faltering heavily in my mind on the inerrancy and sole authority of the Bible, it was not replaced with something else, so I used fuzzy language. The nature of the church was a simple assembly of baptized Bible believing people. At every fiscal quarter churches should practice the two symbolic ordinances of baptism and the Lord's supper. A biblically sound church would show the marks of the present dispensation and work of the Holy Spirit, (no miracles, no speaking in tongues or healing services, just conversions.)

Worship or *Ministering* (liturgizing), consisted of two or three hymnal songs, a special music number pulling at the heart strings sung to a music track. A forty-five minute sermon exegeting the minutia of a biblical text and at least one reference to a word in Greek for spiritual illumination and always, always an altar call to ask people to get saved by asking Jesus into their hearts.

In adult Sunday school classes I would make sure U.S. foreign policy would be included in any study of the book of Revelation. The imminent return of the Lord would be emphasized as just around the corner every time peace in the Middle East was threatened. Any minute God could rapture the true believers to heaven, then seven years of horrible cosmic tribulation under the reign of the Antichrist (usually a Russian political figure or possibly Clinton), leading to

---

[35] Seven worldwide councils (325-787) from both East and West regions of the Roman Empire where the doctrines and teachings of Christianity were detailed and agreed upon by every Christian everywhere or you were a heretic.

Armageddon and then *the end of the world as we know it*. (Insert rock band REM's song)

On my own, I still read Church history and wondered how a seminary could have such intentional amnesia about Church history. I was taught when evil Constantine legalized the tolerance of Christianity with the Edict of Milan, (313 A.D.) true Christianity plunged into the dark ages. I learned about the Inquisitions and abuses of the Roman Catholic Church and there was one page that described Eastern Orthodox Christianity. My church history survey class glossed over twelve hundred years of Church history dismissing them in a couple cursory lectures. There was just the 'badness' of medieval Catholicism to be discovered in those centuries and therefore less relevant to modern Christians.

But we read several volumes about how God righted the path, the biblically based 'new era' apostle saved us again; when Martin Luther nailed his 95 theses to a door in 1517. It was finally time for the true believers to take over with the Protestant Reformation. Recreate an 'invisible church'[36] where two or three could gather and Jesus would be pre-

---

[36] The invisible church is a theological concept of an "invisible" body of the elect who are known only to God, in contrast to the "visible church"— that is, the institutional body on earth which preaches the gospel and administers the sacraments. The concept was insisted upon during the Protestant Reformation as a way of distinguishing between the "visible" Roman Catholic Church, and those within it who truly believe, as well as true believers within the different branches of the every splitting Reformation movement. Both Roman Catholicism and Eastern Orthodoxy proved the theological concept of an "invisible" church as rooted in a long condemned heresy called Nestorianism at the First Council of Ephesus in 431

sent.[37] As long as those two or three were unified by mental agreement of a well-reasoned theological doctrinal statement and a code of conduct of culturally subjective applications of the Bible.

What really happened to me was another spiritual schizophrenic split. The party boy had grown quiet, no longer a voice heard in my head but the preacher boy, like an ameba split in two. A scholarly seminary Christian identity and a practical ministry-leader Christian identity were constantly at odds with each other in my head and life.

It is hard to imagine and explain unless you are deep in the throes of both and unable to bring harmony to the two Christian world views. One valued precise biblical interpretation, detailed doctrinal statements, and codes of conduct cloning versions of outwardly perfect Christians. The other Christian world view valued a more culturally sensitive and inclusive application of broader Christian teachings to those who couldn't clone well or didn't clone well because of sin. (Alcoholics, divorcees, homosexuals, tax collectors, lepers, wine bibbers, feet kissing whores or just your everyday sinner that passed by the Temple because they were too busy trying to make a buck to survive in this world)

Just like Protestantism as a whole, I was divided, conflicted and gripped my Bible so tight my mind could not be opened to think beyond my own personal salvation and that dreaded fear of hell.

---

[37] "For where two or three gather in my name, there am I with them" (Matthew 18:19-21).

I decided to go part-time for the next semester of seminary. I was stalling the next life stage of actually pastoring
other people—of caring for their souls. I told myself I was in
a 'process', on a theological journey. But I was a coward,
lacked conviction, succumbed to the massive and crushing
pressure of acting like the right kind of cloned Christian to
interview and get a job in a congregation.[38] Once again I was
thrust into an ethical dilemma of existential craziness and
doubt.

The Christianity I was subjectively assembling from John
Calvin and the other reformers or the contemporary theologians I studied at seminary was not the Christianity I was
experiencing at the mega-church where I was interning. The
theology I learned about had little practical application in the
life of the mega-church. The nice church type people who all
believed the same things theologically and acted in accordance
with my conservative biblical applications were not what I
saw in the local church ministry that I was required to be
involved with at the seminary.

The goal in the mega-church model was not to define oneself by doctrinal or theological viewpoints. It was to 'encourage people in the Lord' and create ministry programs around
people's similar life stages or relationship predicaments, like
divorcees or single parenting.

---

[38] Seminary grads would go and 'candidate' in congregations. We would
preach a couple of times, be interviewed, and asked to provide biblically
backed answers of how a Christian should live and participate in society. If
you were selected by way of vote then it was deemed 'God's will'.

Due to this theological and practical disconnect, I thought maybe I was too heavenly minded for any earthly good. So I decided to focus on *living* Christianity out rather than *thinking* it out and trying to figure out where someone would theologically best fit in a congregation. 'Church is a verb' my beatnik dread locked friend once said.

I poured myself into some small group ministries and men's accountability groups—the mega-church model for intimate spirituality. My friends and I were consumed with what could be called 'experiencing God'. We set out on a mission to figure out what it meant to give our whole heart to Christ, to be 'dangerously devoted' to Jesus. We would sing hours of praise songs, bring in famous contemporary Christian music artists and hold retreats upon retreats and services upon services desperately trying to experience God. We would share our sins and failings with each other in hopes that this would bring about repentance so we could be holy men of God. We would go on short term mission trips and try to transplant this spirituality in other countries.

Many of us grew disenfranchised with the mega-church model, and wanted to start a new 'reformation'—a reformation of the American Church. My assassination skills were employed again as I began to deconstruct the American mega-church and small group model. The very thing I had hoped would bring me closer to God—to *live* out my Christianity with some sort of authenticity.

My spiritual head injuries had turned into a type of delu-
sional split personality. I had three very different types of
Christians in me. I wanted to be the Baptist preacher boy with
all my theology and biblical interpretations on par with the
tradition that could offer me a career and future ministry. But
Baptist theology didn't matter in the mega-church.

The second type of Christian in me—the 'living it out'
Christian consisted of me helping to organize and lead
modern, culturally hip worship services and programs. I
facilitated and participated in small groups that felt like
biblical therapy sessions. I also went on mission trips to save
Jamaicans and supported others to go to Russia and save the
Orthodox youth from the dead religion of their grandparents.

The third type of Christian in me was in love with historic
Christianity before the Reformation. There was a select group
within some of our small groups that wanted to delve deep
into church history. One of my friends, who had gone
through the same Baptist seminary gauntlet as I did and was an
Episcopalian, spoke strange and scandalous words to me
concerning historic Christianity. Words about how the
Eucharist was as intimate as sex. He said that the apostolic
authority given by Jesus Christ to forgive sins had been passed
down and was available in the sacrament of confession. He
opened up another world to us with stories about monastic
spirituality, and a way to understand the Bible as it had been
interpreted by all Catholic and Eastern Orthodox Christians
throughout history—like a massive study Bible with footnotes
by actual saints.

It was the first time I had ever heard a positive description of Catholicism or Eastern Orthodoxy. His words proved to be soul honey and I drooled for more. I knew then that I would have to go deeper, farther into the rabbit hole of the ancient, sacramental and historical Christian traditions. I would have to learn what it meant to be a Christian and how a 'personal relationship with Jesus' was lived out before Martin Luther.

I had come to the end of the manifestations of Protestant Christianity and found it fractured beyond repair or reform and surely too big to fail. It was certainly full of good, God fearing and loving people. But Protestantism was dying the death of a thousand cuts. Every denomination, congregation and individual tried to stop the bleeding with theological systems of understanding the Bible or life improvement programs to prolong their tradition for at least their lifetime. But it had decapitated itself from the ancient mind of the Church, from its wisdom and from its life giving practices, traditions and sacraments.

The only church and Christianity I knew had forgotten and rejected where it had come from. Protestantism had thrown out the baby with the bath water. It was in a constant state of redefining, explaining, justifying and ardently protesting its very existence against its ancient parentage. It was an angry, rebellious, and dying child of the pope. I finally recognized the breathing tubes, bandages, and the morphine drip of the Protestant life support system I was having trouble plugging into. But I didn't know what to do.

I met with my seminary advisor and discussed all these theological conflicts because it was time to sign the seminary's doctrinal statement again. It was required by every seminary student to sign this before each semester and especially those nearing graduation. I told him I had some bad experiences with signing documents that I did not agree with.

He told me that we are all on theological journeys but I was going down the wrong road with my ecclesiology[39] and thoughts about a sacramental Christianity. He said that if I didn't think I could study under the umbrella of the Reformation/Baptist tradition, sign the doctrinal statement with integrity or pastor a flock in this biblically reasoned way then maybe I should study religion at Michigan State University. He pulled the plug for me and I realized I was in purgatory.[40]

∞

I did not enroll in the last semester to complete my degree at seminary. The preacher boy had finally died. I couldn't figure out why the Baptist flavor of Protestant Christianity did not work for me. I wanted it to. I longed to belong, to be a good and faithful servant of the Lord, but the whole worldview seemed too fabricated. It seemed when it came to biblical interpretation, theology and application we were evolutionist—trying to come up with the most culturally relevant evolution of modern Christianity. Seminary professors, biblical scholars and even my fellow seminarians didn't even agree about what the Bible taught or how to apply it in

---

[39] The branch of theology that is concerned with the nature, constitution, and functions of a church.

[40] Purgatory is a Catholic teaching that when a person dies there is an intermediate state of purification that takes place in the soul to prepare for an eternity with God.

the culture.

I grew uncomfortable and really frightened with the thought of being a care-taker of souls with just a KJV-Ryrie study Bible, a Masters of Divinity degree and a nice Sunday suit. I was too spiritually wounded to trust my personal interpretations and applications of the Bible and those of the theologians that I agreed with and call that biblical Christianity worthy of saving someone's soul from hell.

My wife came home from a night out with friends one evening and I had all my seminary books in boxes.

She asked me what I was doing.

I told her, holding back a torrent of emotions, that I had all the wrong books. I had just finished a book by an Orthodox priest and balled my eyes out. It was so beautiful and it's what I knew to be true, but just had never read it anywhere—I have read all the wrong books.

I wept.

I then told her I was sorry but I couldn't do this type of Christian thing anymore. It wasn't true. I had been manipulated by well-intentioned men from the very beginning and the truth was that I had wasted my whole education.

She had been watching this train derail for a while. She came over to me and hugged me. She knew her embrace was all the support I needed.

I went to a local Christian used bookstore and brought my boxes of books in to be valued and re-shelved in the used book section. The inventory clerk separated them like Jesus

Christ will do with sheep and the goats at the end of time.[41]

"I'll take these off your hands but the other ones won't sell," he said.

I left the bookstore with one box full of books that were used to teach me the truth of God but were not commercially viable to the broader Protestant world. I threw them in the dumpster of our apartment complex.

I had wagered, turned every spiritual fixture in my 'house' upside down and was still hungry to find an authentic, real experience of God. I had grown cynical of Christian institutions, preachers and the commercialization of God. I still had spiritual hunger cramps for some other expression of Christianity or a different spiritual path to live out because I was starving on the emotional roller coaster of it all. I obviously was suffering from some serious spiritual head injuries.

Maybe I would go to hell. Maybe I had lost my salvation or was corrupted by the devil through higher education and liberal theologies. Maybe it was always about me playing an inauthentic role in Christianity, a steady paycheck and trying to work off a debt I thought I owed God for all the sins and ways I hurt other people. Spiritual head injuries really mess a person up.

∞

I decided to learn how to work, manual labor style, in an effort to get me out of this mental prison of contradictions I

---

[41] Matthew 25:31-46 records a parable of Jesus where He separates people into two groups at the end of time. One group are sheep and go to be with Him; the other group are called goats are do not go to be with Him.

had found myself in. So I traded in my KJV for a commercial lawn mower, a weed whacker, hours of AM political talk radio indoctrination and a perennial case of summer long poison ivy.

After a summer or two, I grew tired of that and resurrected my biblical assassination skills of looking at every opportunity to save some poor soul and tweaked it to look at every opportunity to sell someone something. I entered the cut throat world of real estate sales.

The similarities in marketing and negotiating the fine points of a buy-sell agreement with evangelizing and doctrinal statement debates were unsettling. I had become another person again on the outside but spiritually I was still a mess and bitter on the inside. I felt like an old rodeo bull with the rope they tie around the groin of the apathetic bull that has all but given up on life, but still snorts and bucks because the rodeo has him by the balls.

It wasn't clear if I should just be Catholic, Orthodox or Episcopalian. I decided to go slow and figure out how to be 'Catholic-lite'. I would try to live out the old practices of Christianity inside the current American Protestant tradition. Maybe I could be the 'light and salt'[42] and somehow give Protestantism the rodeo ride of her life.

---

[42] "You are the salt of the earth; but if the salt loses its flavor, how shall it be seasoned? It is then good for nothing but to be thrown out and trampled underfoot by men. "You are the light of the world. A city that is set on a hill cannot be hidden. Nor do they light a lamp and put it under a basket, but on a lampstand, and it gives light to all who are in the house…" (Matthew 5:13-16).

Most of me wanted to give up on the Bible, God and Christianity, but I couldn't. Probably out of guilt or fear of hell. They have always been effective motivators for me. Plus, when someone wagers with God the way I did, at the high roller table, it was impossible to fold and walk away. It usually meant major changes in spiritual scenery. I remembered my time at St. Patrick's on Parnell Road, reminded God of our old wagers and grew slowly fearful of where God was leading me.

My prayers were more like begging God to not give up on me and to forgive my brutal assassinations on the people I had now come to realize were fellow pilgrims. They were all better Christians than I was. I also knew it would get lonely on the long dark road of unlearning God the more I talked about sacraments and the historical church and less about literal biblical interpretation and lifestyle applications or codes of conduct. But I had to continue on and see it through to its end. I clung to one verse; "Draw near to God and He will draw near to you" (James 4: 8a). It sounded like a wager to me.

CATECHUMENS DEPART

I was convinced Protestant Christianity in America was broken. At least it wasn't working for me. My friend and I thought we could breathe new life into Protestantism with the ancient practices of Christianity—a new reformation by way of pre-reformational Christianity.

We had ideas about how we were going to start a new movement; 'cell-churches' or 'house-churches' that included Catholic-Orthodox type disciplines, like fasting and confession. The goal was to get back to how we thought 'church' was done in the book of Acts. However, we were experiencing a backlash from many people and parents claiming that what we taught was a type of 'neo-sacramentalism' or too Catholic. We held an Ash Wednesday teen night service during lent and had more frequent and modern forms of communion rituals.

One time my friend and I served communion at a youth event using potato chips and Pepsi. We knew the act of communion was special but thought the elements could be anything. The hope was that every time the teens drank Pepsi or ate potato chips they would think of the death and resurrection of Christ—a way to bring Jesus into the twentieth century.

As we were cleaning up after the service—with oily and

salty fingers, taking random shots of soda pop and throwing away the little cups I said, "Maybe we are doing this wrong and if we are, we're in big trouble." We both nervously smiled at each other and then I took the trash bag filled with symbolic Jesus out to the dumpster.

We had been talking to our Episcopalian friend for several months and were continuously seduced and scandalized by the Eastern Orthodox books he was reading. We wanted to see this stuff in action. Books were nice but how was it 'lived out' and would it 'play' in a new Protestant expression of worship became our interest.

We found out that Patriarch Bartholomew, the Ecumenical Patriarch of Eastern Orthodox Christianity was visiting America and had decided to visit near my friend's home town of all places. We decided to take a road trip to Iowa.

The service wasn't in an Orthodox Church but an auditorium and it was some sort of weird chanting service with guys in black robes and a man with a big black hat with other people kissing his hand. I sat in the back and cynically observed. I had my sniper scope focused just for fun. We left thinking one thing; we would not become Orthodox because neither of us looked good in hats and no one should kiss another man's hands.

However, we were intrigued by the claim that Orthodoxy was the 'true Church'. So we tried to research as much as we could about Orthodoxy after our visit to Iowa, but there was little out there. In the late nineties the Internet was in its infancy and AOL had started to charge for disks and hours on the Internet. We were forced to go to the second most reliable source of free information—the phone book.

Lo and behold there were Orthodox churches right here in Grand Rapids, Michigan. We both looked at each other in sheer amazement because the phone book was actually useful and partly because we had no idea of their existence in our very religiously tainted town. Grand Rapids is a hot-bed of Protestant Christendom: Four major Christian publishing companies; four Christian colleges, (five if you counted the Catholic College) three Protestant seminaries, the world headquarters of the Christian Reformed Church and Amway, (wait that might not be a denomination) several mega-churches and more churches than restaurants in the city. (I counted one year)

We wanted to go to a service but with teaching duties at the current church it was impossible to go on a Sunday morning. We needed to see the mysterious Divine Liturgy, where supposedly myriads of invisible angels worshipped.

My friend said, "Let's give them a call and see what happens."

We called Holy Trinity Greek Orthodox Church. The call was answered by a gentleman—not the priest. We started to ask questions about services and icons.[43] We both were drawn to icons, with their curiously flat and dark toned hues. They

---

[43] Distinctive formulistic images of Christ, saints, feasts and other events in the Bible. They adorn the walls and ceilings in Orthodox Church buildings and homes of her faithful. They are usually lit by oil lamps or candles and are used as teaching tools and prayer aides. The 7th ecumenical council universally claimed their validity, use from the beginning of the Church and veneration as proper for worshipping the Divinity represented in the image, not worshipping the image itself.

were very different from the Protestant 'icons' we knew: The good looking, movie star, soft glowing and long hair flowing Jesus pictures, the old man praying over a loaf of bread or, the beach picture of footprints with that awful poem that hung in businesses to secretly let their customers know they were a Christian company.

"How can we buy an icon?" I asked over the speaker phone.

"Why do you want an icon?" he asked back.

"Um, I'm not sure but are they for sale? I'm willing to buy one."

"What will you do with an icon if I sell you one?" he asked.

There was a long pause as my friend and I looked at each other, neither with an answer. I wondered why this guy was not more helpful. The Orthodox Church was certainly not 'seeker friendly' at first engagement.

"I don't know, we'll hang it up on a wall—can we buy one?" I asked with a slight tone.

"We don't sell them," he said.

We ended our conversation with him, puzzled by this interaction but something else was awakened in me. A small seed of entitlement or pissed off'ness was planted in my soul. What is so valuable over there that I can't even buy an icon? What are they protecting or hiding? *I want an icon, dammit!* I know they sell them but he didn't want to sell one to me. Why?

We called another church—St. John Chrystostom's Russian Orthodox Church. No one answered the phone but there was a recording which informed us about a *daily* Liturgy served at nine in the morning. More than an icon, we really wanted to go to an actual Orthodox service and see for ourselves. We both looked at each other in unspoken resolved agreement that we would go the next day.

By now we had read everything available to us about Orthodoxy and knew it claimed to be the original Church. This claim alerted us and piqued our curiosity because that's what we wanted to reboot—the beliefs and practices of the early Church, that dynamic group we had read about in the book of Acts. We were obsessed with the book of Acts chapter 2 as it described—agape feasts, singing, praising God with spiritual hymns, breaking bread, reading the memoirs of the apostles.

We wanted to get back to the beginning, to the grass roots of what Jesus started. I wanted to figure out what the Apostles were actually doing when they 'planted' churches on all those missionary journeys mapped out with colorful lines in the back of Bibles. If I could be involved with a movement like that then I hoped my 'Christian life' would be real, verifiably connected to the work of the Holy Spirit and have a semblance of authenticity.

I also hoped I would stop feeling embarrassed by the 'pop culture Christianity' that was mimicking everything from rock-n-roll music trends, to T-shirts with product brand gospel propaganda screen-printed on them, to coffee shop ambience—there were new 'espresso ministries' with fully equipped coffee bars popping up in mega-church vestibules everywhere.

We believed the stage was being set for the next great

revival or 'Great Awakening'[44] to catch fire with us at the helm. It looked positive. I had a flicker of excitement and a spark of hope. Except for this crazy thing called Orthodoxy with its boastful claims of being the original and unchanged Church throughout history. The claims had to be dealt with, analyzed and assassinated because it looked too odd, too Catholic and more like an ethnic social organization for Greeks, Russians and whatever an Antiochian was. It could not be the Church, the "real" Church of the book of Acts. We needed to experience it and I, with my biblical assassin skills, needed to shoot it down.

Protestants are rarely late for church services, so we showed up at eight forty-five in the morning. The church building was in a beaten down part of town, mostly rentals and the forgotten memory of Polish immigrants on rusted signs and social halls. The white siding and blue spiral dome marked the building as a converted house of sorts. A 'house-church'— I was able to assimilate this humble building into my concept of the true 'church' we had hoped to re-start.

I checked my watch because the service seemed to have

---

[44] In 18th century and the late 19th century historians describe three or four mass movements in America of increased religious enthusiasm in the. Each of these "Great Awakenings" was characterized by widespread revivals led by evangelical Protestant ministers, a sharp increase of interest in religion, a profound sense of conviction and redemption on the part of those affected, an increase in evangelical church membership, and the formation of new religious movements and denominations.

started but no one was there. We walked up to the doors; no greeters present. There was a type of vestibule, with a large icon of St. John Chrysostom, whom we knew nothing about. A booth was to our right where dark yellow candles of various sizes were for sale. There was a box and price list—the honor system; I liked this. There were some pamphlets and literature similar to what I'd seen at St. Patrick's Catholic Church years earlier but thankfully no coffee bar ministry in sight.

In front of us were two light blue doors that were on swinging hinges with automatic pull back springs. There was a crack between the two doors and we could see the dark room. Red-glassed candles flickered in circular candle stands. There was a huge floor to ceiling white wall with icons, candles and spot lights on it. We were bold and walked through the doors.

Unprepared for the assault on our senses we drifted to the side. No pews, no lights, no projector screen for praise songs, just icons—icons everywhere, all over the walls, on the columns and even up the stairs. A huge icon of Mary and baby Jesus painted on the East wall that dominated the whole room. Clouds of incense hovered like fog, icons of angels and gaunt faced people randomly hung on the walls, but no people and no praise band. Just a young woman who sang in a beautiful alto voice with her head covered and a priest vested in purple and gold. He was quite busy, moving in and out of doors and around the center altar. Passages of Scripture made their way to my mind:

Isaiah 6:1-8

"In the year that King Uzziah died, I saw the **Lord sitting on a throne, high and lifted up**, and the **train of His** *robe* **filled the temple**. [2] Above it stood **seraphim**; each one had six wings: with two he covered his face, with two he covered his feet, and with two he flew. [3] And one cried to another and said:

" **Holy, holy, holy** *is* **the LORD of hosts**;
 The whole earth *is* full of His glory!"

[4] And the **posts of the door** were shaken by the voice of him who cried out, and **the house was filled with smoke**.

[5] So I said: "Woe *is* me, for I am undone! Because I *am* a man of unclean lips, And I dwell in the midst of a people of unclean lips; For my eyes have seen the King, The LORD of hosts."

[6] Then one of the **seraphim flew to me**, having in his hand a **live coal** *which* **he had taken with the tongs from the altar.** [7] And he touched my mouth *with it,* and said:

" Behold, this has touched your lips; Your iniquity is taken away, and your sin purged."

[8] Also I heard the voice of the Lord, saying:

" Whom shall I send, and who will go for us?"
Then I said, "Here *am* I! Send me."

First Corinthians 11:13

"Judge among yourselves. Is it proper for a woman to pray to God with **her head uncovered**?

Hebrews 12:1

"Therefore we also, since we are **surrounded by so great a cloud of witnesses**, let us lay aside every weight, and the sin which so easily ensnares us, and let us run with endurance the race that is set before us."

It was like the Bible coming to life. I was confused, elated, enchanted, skeptical and yet I knew I would never go back to what I thought was worshipping God, again. It was other worldly; I just didn't know which planet I was on.

I leaned over to my friend and said, "We're not in Kansas anymore, Toto."

He smiled and said, "No we are not."

Then something happened that we did not expect. The priest came out a side door with a smoking silver ball on a chain and started yo-yoing it all around—he tossed it then jerked it back and puffs of smoke wafted out. He did this to all the icons on the great white wall, the icons on the side walls, on the columns, then to the head-covered singer and then he started after us.

He walked towards us mumbling words we couldn't make out and shook the canister of fire and smoke at us. We moved out of his way quickly. He shook it three times and swung it almost three hundred and sixty degrees to get some icons on the back of a column. Then he came after us again. He was careful to not make eye contact. The woman sang in a most haunting tone. The priest shook the tumbler of smoke at us and we moved again. *He is chasing us! Why is he chasing us?* I was freaked out.

The pursuit relented and he went back through the other hidden door with an angel holding a sword on it. I felt safe again. I laughed nervously and shook my head because I did not get what was going on.

Soon he repositioned himself behind the white wall and started to 'sing-song' back and forth with the young woman. 'Lord have mercy' was her response to what sounded like verses from a hundred different psalms. I stood in the back and tried to make sense of it all.

We stood for a long time, before I heard the priest say in a loud voice, "All ye catechumens, depart! Depart, ye cate-chumens! All ye that are catechumens depart! Let no cate-chumens remain! But let us who are of the faithful, again and again, in peace pray to the Lord."

I recognized this word, *catechumen*. I ran across it in some reading. It meant a student or learner of the faith. I looked to my buddy and said, "Should we leave?" He was silent. The priest seemed to pause, so we both slipped through the doors into the vestibule.

We quietly whispered about how funny it was to be chased with fire and how no one else had come to the service. We stood out in the vestibule and soon realized that it was not heated and it was February in Michigan. I was cold. I wanted so badly to have a cup of warm coffee and immediately had new respect for espresso bar ministries.

My friend wanted to leave the service and go back to the church offices but I couldn't—I wouldn't, that was simply not an option for me. There was too much I had seen. Now the priest had asked us to leave—no, ordered us to 'depart'. We stood outside in the cold, hands under our armpits; we paced and watched our breath materialize into moisture. We took turns peeking through the swinging door gap for about a half hour. We saw the priest come out with a gold cup and spoon but no one to feed. He then went back busily about his tasks. We were freezing.

I thought about how I was denied the purchase of an icon and now kicked out of a service. How can this be the all welcoming Church of Christ? Certainly the Lord, who was shunned from the 'inn' when He was born, would allow me, a seeker of truth who had wagered everything to start a new reformation, to be inside this crazy unattended Orthodox service. He surely wouldn't send me out of a service without telling me why. That was not part of our wager system— clear directions!

Orthodoxy at first experience didn't seem right—too exclusive. Why was I kicked out? I was an American! I was a seminary student! I was a Bible believing Christian, baptized twice and saved by the blood of Christ on the Cross! I was zealous for the Lord and I was going to restart the church and turn the world upside down, just like it was said of the apostles in the book of Acts.[45] Yet, here I stood outside, not included in the most ancient form of Christian worship with no one really attending the service.

I realized for the first time how severe the spiritual head injuries of my pride and self-centeredness were. I was left out in the cold, separated from any tangible connection to the historical and real expression of a Christian life. My version of Christianity had devolved into an exclusive mental mixture of 'chapter and verse' biblical proof texts, hodge-podge theological assassination straw-man arguments and middle class melancholy. Now God with His ancient Church worship didn't want me in the room.

Eventually we re-entered the warmness and the sweet smell of the nave. The priest greeted us. He was friendly and soft spoken. I no longer feared him chasing me around with the ball of fire. He asked why we left and stood outside— perhaps he offended us with something he said in his brief sermon.

I laughed and said, "You said, 'all catechumens depart' and I didn't know if we are catechumens officially but it felt like the right thing to do."

He smiled and said, "I'm glad people still listen to the Liturgy."

We talked for a half hour or so about Lent and Orthodoxy. He was obviously perplexed at our many odd questions but he was so gracious and invited us back to any service we

---

[45] "But when they did not find them, they dragged Jason and some brethren to the rulers of the city, crying out, 'These who have turned the world upside down have come here too'" (Acts 17:6).

wanted to attend. He turned to leave when he looked back over his shoulder and said, "You can stay inside for the whole service next time. It's cold out there."

∞

Stories from the Bible and many of the saints record that when a great sinner encounters great holiness or virtue it can lead to great repentance and that is what happened to me that day. [46] I realized that I had been blinded by my cynicism and all the wonderful things I was going to do for the Lord. It wasn't until I saw God being truly worshipped that I recognized Him, even with all my biblical knowledge, seminary education, preaching and teaching and 'theologizing' about God. I realized that it was only my personal and flawed interpretations of God that I believed. I was a man of 'unclean lips', like Isaiah. I lacked knowledge of how to approach God in humility. I just wanted to be used by God in some amazing way but my schizophrenic 'living it out' Christianity and my militant biblical theology were still very much about me being the last assassin standing in the shoot out of Protestant Christianity.

My 'clear direction' wager requirement with God had taken a sharp left eastward. Now my divine 'wagers' would have little to do with what I judged as an acceptable Christian life, or about what I thought I could do for the Lord as a pastor or leader in cutting edge emergent movements of Christianity. After that day I knew I would have to leave

---

[46] Ref. Isaiah Chapter 6, St. Mary of Egypt or St. Moses the Ethiopian

behind the quest of personally reforming Christianity with my self-created versions of an 'authentic' Christian life. Instead of raising my fist in the air demanding things of God, like on that dock when I was in high school, I would now find my soul continually at a knife's edge cutting away at my infected spiritual head injuries.

There was no turning back for me now. I had seen the Lord high and lifted up, seated on a throne and the train of His robe had filled the temple of my heart. I was alive inside. I had finally had my mystical encounter with God that I had longed for since I was sitting on the dock. I was truly 'undone' like Isaiah.[47]

My wife and I started to attend as many services at St. Nicholas Antiochian Eastern Orthodox Church as we could. We had met with the priest several times and I spilled my guts to him. We attended as many services as were offered, keeping one foot in the small group communities on Sunday mornings at the mega-church to see if anyone was going to come with us. Eventually some people did hint at possibly moving with us, but wanted to go slowly and maybe even as a group. But when we were invited to start the process of joining Orthodoxy by the priest; I couldn't say, no.

I had to leave behind Protestant Christianity, the small

---

[47] "Woe is me, for I am undone! Because I am a man of unclean lips, And I dwell in the midst of a people of unclean lips; For my eyes have seen the King, The LORD of hosts" (Isaiah 6:5).

groups and sadly many friendships and family relationships were strained. I was no longer asked to pray at family dinners and from Promise Keepers[48] to politics, my opinions were no longer sought after. Instead of being asked to pray for someone, I was put on those 'prayer lists'. This was not supposed to happen to Baptist boys, like me. I was trained to convert people to a personal relationship with Jesus and belief in a Bible-only Christianity not be converted to a crazy Catholic-looking ethnic religion. This was surely the work of demons some people said to me.

But I had experienced the inexplicable mystery of God's all burning love. I finally experienced God—the burning bush, the pillar of fire, Jacob's wrestler, the slaying of Goliath, the love of Hosea for the whore, the fearful thunder and gentle dove at the Baptism, the mental freedom of the demoniac and the swine, the stone that got rolled away, the angelic earthquake that broke the prison doors. Like a moth to the flame, drawn to the light and the pain, I would now keep myself in the crucible of being in a sacramental and personal relationship with His holy and historically instituted Orthodox Church—the visible Body of Christ. I would have to unlearn everything I thought I knew about God, the Bible, salvation, the 'Christian life' and His 'Church'.

---

[48] Promise Keepers is an international conservative Christian organization for men. It is a non-profit organization, not affiliated with any Christian church or denomination started in 1990. While it originated in the United States, it is now world-wide. It is self-described as a Christ-centered organization dedicated to introducing men to Jesus Christ as their Savior and Lord, helping them to grow as Christians.

Soon I would confess all my sins to the priest instead of my pillow. I would be asked to recite the entire Nicene Creed without adaptation and as an authoritative guide for my theology. I would be anointed on my head, eyes, ears, mouth, hands and feet with holy oil (chrism) and sealed with the Holy Spirit literally instead of emotionally at some Pentecostal praise fest. I would soon partake of the mysteriously transformed Body/bread and Blood/wine in the holy Eucharist, those physical/spiritual life-giving and *healing* sacraments.

Soon I would be sacramentally joined to the historic Eastern Orthodox Church and a member at the local parish of St. Nicholas Antiochian Orthodox Church. I took the invitation to join Orthodoxy from the Antiochian priest as a clear direction from God because it was in Antioch that people were first called 'Christians', (Acts 11:26) and only a retired biblical assassin would know that verse by heart.

It seemed God had raised the pot on our wager, changed my spiritual scenery and now asked me if I was really 'all-in' with this whole Christian life wager thing we had going on.

I was.

PRE-REFORMATIONAL
CHRISTIAN MAN
IN HIS NATURAL HABITAT

A month before we were asked to join Eastern Orthodoxy, a couple of evangelical thinking men from St. Nicholas Antiochian Orthodox Church caught wind that a small group of Protestants were sniffing around the Orthodox churches in town. These men extended an invitation to come hear the famous Campus Crusade convert to Orthodoxy, Fr. Peter Gillquist, and hear him talk about missionary work in the Orthodox Church.

Now for people who have come from Protestantism to Orthodoxy, Fr. Peter is like a grandfather.[49] The story of him and his hundreds of sojourners making their way to Orthodoxy in the seventies has risen to an epic tale almost equal to Pentecost. I had made it a priority to have at least one copy of his book, <u>Becoming Orthodox</u>, and several brochures based on the book, to give out to my Protestant friends when they

---

[49] During the final editing of this memoir Fr. Peter Gillquist passed away. May his memory be eternal. I know he will be in my memory for eternity. I had the blessing of talking with him personally several times and his book was a constant reminder that we were fellow sojourners in many ways. The lasting effect of his book on me was another 'divine prompting' and encouragement for me to write this memoir. He was a wonderful man.

would take issue with what the Orthodox Church taught. In the back of my mind I hoped reading his book would somehow magically convert them because it was too tempting for me get in a debate about biblical interpretation or theology and assassinate them.

The event was great for me because missionary work had always tugged at my heart and I wondered how the Orthodox Church did this kind of thing. Fr. Peter spoke with the same cadence that I recognized as, 'good ol' fashioned preachin'. I can't remember what he actually spoke about, but what I do remember is the question and answer part of the talk.

One of the inviting gentlemen, named Clement (Clem), was on the committee that brought Fr. Peter in to speak. He also arranged a special time for some of us to speak with Fr. Peter later, so I wasn't sitting in the front row with loaded questions challenging the speaker's knowledge of the Bible or ready to argue a point of doctrine. Biblical assassins normally do this at these types of events. I had been 'that guy' at St. Patrick's in my college days. I think we can all admit that nobody likes 'confrontation question guy'.

Someone asked Fr. Peter why he hadn't started a church in Thief River Falls, Minnesota. This was a seemingly harmless question of which Fr. Peter answered but the person kept going on about how their children and grandchildren had no Orthodox church to go to in Thief River Falls.

Fr. Peter graciously deflected the accusatory tone that it was somehow his fault but this person would not let it go. Personal 'angst' from this person was working itself out on Fr. Peter. Most meetings have that one person that goes too far or asks that one personal angst question of a speaker and will not give up without an acceptable answer. I've been that guy too. Again I think we can admit that, nobody likes 'angst question guy' either.

The room grew uncomfortable so I got up from my seat and looked for a refill of the bad tasting coffee when Clem approached me. I could tell he was nervous about what all of us must be thinking about this part of the meeting. The Thief River Falls debate was escalating to embarrassing levels. He had worked so hard at welcoming us to St. Nicholas and genuinely wanted us to join Orthodoxy.

I managed to get my hands on a cup of the brown liquid laced with undissolved powdered creamer and stood in the back and listened to the woes of Thief River Falls; it sounded like Sodom and Gomorrah. 'Angst questioner' was now flatly accusing Fr. Peter, head of the Archdiocesan mission department, of not making it a priority to start a mission parish in Thief River Falls. The whole room was groaning at this exchange and there was no good end in sight. Everybody looked at their watches and wanted the meeting to end. Nervous that all his efforts would be soured by this exchange, Clem leaned over to me and said, "I don't know what the hell that person's talking about."

I smiled for several reasons. First because he said, 'hell' and it felt like swearing in church, very naughty. Secondly, because I sensed he really wanted us to feel welcomed at St. Nicholas and hoped that the magic of Fr. Peter would convert all of us. What he didn't know was that I was already 'all in' and that the hospitality of his heart had won me over. The 'swearing' added a touch of authenticity to his personality. This was a real guy living out his faith, not trying to 'present' a false piety. What you saw with Clem is what you got and I loved it.

People have often asked me, why I chose to join the parish of St. Nicholas over the other parishes in town. This is a truly awful question to answer because it seems like you're saying something bad about the other parishes. But truth be told, Clem and his wife welcomed all of us and especially me with sincerity exuding from their hearts. He was a 'special greeter' to those of us who were coming to see what Fr. Peter found so long ago now. I really needed a 'special greeter' at that time. I needed for someone to love on me a little bit because I was existentially scared, spiritually wounded with no ministry or career opportunities from my education. I had committed theological treason in Protestant Christendom and was now wandering like Abraham in a strange land called Orthodoxy.

∞

Fast forward several years and a ministry of Clem-like 'special greeters' had taken root at St. Nicholas. Almost every Sunday we get visitors from local colleges that visit the Divine Liturgy. Being Protestants, they are always early of course, and they stand wide-eyed in the vestibule eager to understand what is going on. There is a twinge of horror in their eyes about being late because a service is going on but no people are present. I know this look in their eyes from my first visit to a Divine Liturgy.

It is the job of the 'special greeter' to first tell the group that they are not late, but that this is a shamefully, poorly attended prayer service called matins.[50] Then they officially welcome them to St. Nicholas, give them some pamphlets—based on Fr. Peter's book hoping for some spiritual magic to rub off on them. They are ushered into one pew and usually sit in total bewilderment at Pre-Reformational Christian man in his natural habitat.

For Protestants the ancient Divine Liturgy, over 1700 years old, is something from a different planet: Standing and sitting randomly, with delayed uniformity, a choir seated above and behind the congregation and that grows louder as late-comers sneak into the choir loft, a priest with his back to you almost the entire service, vestments, icons, smoke-billowing censers, multiple languages being chanted, secret pocket doors with mysterious activities behind the icon wall, a group of robed young boys and older clergy making a conga line trip around the back of the pews, people kissing icons, people sitting, standing, kneeling, crossing themselves at all different times, a sermon that is under eight minutes right in the middle of the service and people getting in line to be spoon fed from a large golden cup. Yes, this is Pre-Reformational Christian man in his natural habitat and sadly most Protestants do not recognize it. I didn't. By the end of the service the visitors have several hundred questions.

The Reformation and particularly the Radical Reformation

---

[50] One of the morning prayer services, part of the 'hours' of prayer. The service is held right before Divine Liturgy in most Orthodox Churches worldwide.

as it has evolved over the last couple hundred years, has severely wounded the collective Protestant Christian mind. Protestants don't recognize worship as it was meant to be and when they do see it they protest it as being too 'Catholic' or too close to idol worship.

Having been in recovery from this particular spiritual head injury I can admit that I thought early Christianity was a 'movement' with stringed instruments, bon fires, and singing 'Kum-ba-ya'. To my shock and work of unlearning God, I found out the early Church was liturgical, structured, and hierarchical, a divine/human institution that Jesus started and the Apostles developed in this fashion. It caused a spiritual stroke in me to think that maybe the Apostles worshipped like Catholics. I needed to be healed from a type of Christian historical amnesia, stop protesting the pope and humbly be enlightened about what Christianity looked like before the Reformation, the printing press or even the invention of overhead projection screens.

'Come and see' has become the slogan for Orthodoxy in America but that often leads to spiritual culture shock that 'special greeters' are expected to handle. How does someone explain the fullness of Orthodoxy, liturgical rubrics, the assault on the senses from the incense, icons and vestments and two thousand years of evolving church worship and history in a ten minute Q & A?

I know the special greeters suggest Fr. Peter's 'magic' book or the pamphlets but that takes time to read. Protestants are protesting, biblical assassins are taking aim, Bible verse grenades are being launched. There is too much that can't be minimized to sound bite answers or text message theology.

But that's the 'special greeters' job. On Sundays at St. Nicholas, after communion, the visitors are lead out of the service into a bunker room (chapel) and get to ask hundreds of loaded questions. The 'special greeters' must give Twitter-like answers because that's what time allows.

I was a 'special greeter' for some time but I don't do it anymore. If somebody is seeking out Orthodoxy, I am willing to talk to them. I will even invite them to a cup of coffee for a longer conversation if they want. I think it is wonderful for people to seek out Orthodoxy but within five minutes I will ask, "Have you read Fr. Peter Gillquist's, <u>Becoming Ortho-dox</u>?" I want that magic conversion thing to work. It's so much easier than helping someone unlearn a version of God.

Over the years I have come to believe that you cannot explain Orthodoxy to POST-reformational man in one visit, nor should its hidden life giving mysteries be justified to accommodate biblical proof-texted objections. Often the visitors are unaware of their spiritual injuries and most of the school class trips are mandatory, academically nuanced and filled with people that ask those loaded questions. Many of them remind me of me in my days as a biblical assassin. Nobody likes biblical assassin 'confrontational question' guy or 'angst question' guy. True seekers asking questions, yes, of course they are a joy to talk with. And there are always a few honest 'seekers' struggling to assess their Christian experi-ence, compare their faith tradition against Church history and speculate about their career/ministry options.

Years of that kind of arguing, confronting, skepticism,

questioning, gawking, even disrespectful manners during the Divine Liturgy require a special kind of heart to endure—a virtuous heart. Anger entered my heart one Q & A session when a visiting biblical assassin said that Orthodox worship is just 'an idolatrous theater of spectacle and the traditions of men—Leviticus talks about this type of idolatry'. He had taken his sniper shot from my old arsenal. I soon bowed out of the 'special greeters' ministry. God bless our 'special greeter' ministry but I still go through slight episodes of post traumatic spiritual stress syndrome in these spiritually topical Q and A's.

After that biblical assassination attempt I knew that being a 'special greeter' required the virtue of hospitality to handle those statements week in and week out. I also understood that it's a ministry that plants seeds for a life long journey, a journey I know well. I've been through the reconstructive surgery of joining Orthodoxy as a born and bred American Protestant—it's painful spiritual therapy and it takes so much time to unlearn certain versions of God—some never make it out of the ICU.

Recently, my wife sat in on one of those 'special greeter' Q & A sessions and walked out welled up in tears as I passed by her in the hall. I caught up with her at the coffee hour and asked what happened. She told me that one of the 'special greeters' shared his faith with such humility and sincerity in his heart that it was like watching a saint speak of their love for Christ. The Orthodox tradition is a "saint-maker"—a far superior way to evaluate a branch of Christianity than 'chapter and verse' biblical assaults.

I would much rather talk about how the worship and practice of Orthodox Christianity can heal spiritual injuries and even make someone a saint; or about how the thousands of Orthodox saints who 'lived out' their Christianity by being martyred for doctrines like the Trinity, Divinity of Jesus, role of Mary in our salvation and the veneration[51] of icons. Hell, I'd rather talk about how Orthodoxy has given us hummus, grape leaves, and baklava than listen to prideful sound bite doctrinal arguments and the Bible verse sniper shots from people who haven't unlearned God. It still gives me a spiritual migraine to argue about Orthodoxy with Protestants, so I don't. I don't argue at all about anything spiritual now.

But I've suffered spiritual head injuries and more spiritual healing is something I am still in desperate need of—it takes years to recover. I don't lose hope though. The Orthodox Church, other than being the divinely desired place of worship for Pre-Reformational Christian man and a 'saint-making' tradition is also described by the church fathers as a spiritual hospital.

The parish of St. Nicholas has been that kind of hospital for me. I'm sure it will be for many of the visitors that come almost weekly and experience the virtue of hospitality that our 'special greeters' show. Or maybe they will receive a warm handshake from Deacon Clem or maybe even a kind word from a person like me. I think the virtue of hospitality starts the healing process for those who have suffered spiritual

---

[51] Veneration is an act like kissing or bowing to show respect to the holiness of God represented in physical objects, like icons or crosses.

head injuries. Once you have experienced divine hospitality then you can set down your rifle and have a thankful heart to God and everyone around you. Thankfulness is the first evidence of spiritual healing.

I am very thankful for Metropolitan[52] Philip's thirty year invitation to 'Come and See' Orthodoxy alive and well in America. I am thankful for the spiritual healers I've met— priests, deacons, chanters and laity. I'm thankful for all the 'special greeters' out there that are willing to deal with spiritually injured biblical assassins, like me. But most of all I'm thankful I don't live in Thief River Falls, Minnesota.

---

[52] In Eastern Orthodoxy the rank of metropolitan bishop, or simply metropolitan, pertain to the diocesan bishop or archbishop of a region (or country). Before the establishment of patriarchs (beginning in AD 325), metropolitan was the highest Episcopal rank in the Eastern rites of the Church. They presided over synods of bishops, and were granted special privileges by canon law and sacred tradition.

SLAP THAT HERETIC

I've only hit one other person in my life. I got into a fight at the bus stop one morning as tempers flared between me and another eleven year old. I back-handed a boy named Joe, right in the face for insulting my family. He was taller than me and probably could have taken me down, but the back-handed slap is such a humiliating gesture; I think it shamed him. I love the back-handed slap.

St. Nicholas of Myra is probably one of, if not *the,* most famous saints of all time. We have no written document by him. We have no recorded sermons by him. We do have legendary stories of tremendous virtue, meekness and charity that have evolved into the world-wide Santa Claus myth. But my favorite story about St. Nick was when he threw a haymaker at the Ecumenical Council of Nicaea[53] and shut some slanderer, named Arius, right up.

Now I'm not sure if it was a true haymaker or a backhand-

---

[53] The first of seven Ecumenical Councils the world wide Church held before the split in 1054 between the Greek Eastern and Latin Western branches of Christianity. The seven councils were assembled to defend and define what constituted the true Christian faith and her practices. The proclamations from the seven councils defined what an Christian believed and consequently what a heretic, schismatic and apostate believed.

ed slap St. Nick used but it was enough to land him in prison, stripped of his vestments, left in a cell wearing rags and defrocked as a bishop. Meetings back then were a lot more lively than today. The Theotokos[54] and the Lord visited him in prison and he pleaded his case to them. He said he couldn't listen to one more insulting word being spewed out of that guy's mouth about the Lord. So he shut him up. He slapped that heretic! What a zealous love for Jesus Bishop Nicholas from Myra had.

The next morning he spoke of his divine visitors and explained the vision and that Mary returned his vestments to him. He was let back into the Council. I bet Arius was more cautious about what he said around St. Nicholas from that day on. I know 'back-handed' Joe from my bus stop never said anything about my family again.

∞

Fast forward almost 1700 years to the first General Assembly we attended at our parish after joining the Orthodox Church. My wife and I were young twenty-somethings and we recently had our first child. We had read every single book in English we could get our hands on about life in the

---

[54] An Orthodox title for Mary from the third Ecumenical Council in Ephesus 431. In the debates that define Jesus Christ as truly God and truly man the Greek term Theotokos communicated that. The word means 'Birth-giver of God'. To deny Mary as the Theotokos was to deny the divinity of Jesus. In the Orthodox Liturgies and prayer services this title is used for her. Orthodox Christians commonly refer to her as the Theotokos rather than the Blessed Virgin Mary like the Catholics.

Orthodox Church: <u>Becoming Orthodox</u> by Fr. Peter Gillquist was nearly memorized. <u>The Orthodox Church</u> by Bishop Kallistos (Timothy) Ware was dog eared and the cover was permanently curled up. Fr. Alexander Schmemann's books were a little too advanced for us to truly understand at this stage of acclimating to life in the Orthodox Church but we consumed them all the same. But Frank (Frankie) Schaeffer was my favorite author. He stood up against the tradition I grew up in and told them they were wrong in his early books and again stated this passionately during a taped presentation at Calvin College one year. (Slap) That VHS tape was soon copied and bootlegged all over North America, much like the story of St. Nicholas and Arius must have traveled.

My spiritual head injuries had become infected with anger at my Protestant Christian upbringing and education. Some 'converts' to Orthodoxy look fondly back on their Protestant roots and how it brought them this far. Others don't. Some are pissed off, have some anger issues because they feel they were lied to, deceived, and are spiritually injured. The process of being asked to leave the seminary and any opportunity for a career or ministry for believing the truth understood by Orthodoxy over against the seminary's doctrinal statement was painful and I was bitter. I needed spiritual reconstructive surgery. My old relationships were severed and I took judgmental bullets for getting mixed up with those 'crazy ethnic Catholics' from my family and almost everyone I knew. They thought I believed the traditions of men over the Bible. Those who commit this kind of treason shall be tarred and feathered! I felt like throwing a haymaker at all of

Protestantism but was satisfied with Frank's back-hand.

The annual general assembly took place in the basement after the evening vesper[55] prayer service on a Saturday night. Once a year the parish had a big meeting to handle all the 'business' of the parish. We would now get to see how Orthodox Christians got stuff done. It was well attended because we had a new priest and there had been some sparks flying around the recent coffee hours as the new guy got to know the parish. I won't go into the details because that would be like sharing a family's dirty laundry.

However, I will tell you I had a front row seat when one parishioner stood up and pointed his finger at the priest and yelled, "Are you threatening us Father?" —all sense of parliamentary procedure was lost. It was chaos.

Finally another parishioner was so sick of the behavior he stood up and yelled, "I'll pay for the whole thing, myself!"

'No's' rang out from everywhere and things calmed down a bit. It was the craziest meeting I had ever been to. I had no reference or Bible verse or experience to compare it to. I couldn't walk away from it and I couldn't control it. I had to just live in the paradoxical moment of a divinely established community on the verge of a brawl. Several outbursts by different people gave me the context I needed to understand the intense and even physical rebuke St. Nicholas gave to Arius at Nicaea.

The assembly concluded and I looked over at my wife who

---

[55] One of the evening prayer services, part of the 'hours' of prayer. The service is held nightly in monasteries and every Saturday in North American Antiochian Orthodox parishes.

had started to cry. I was in a slight state of shock, myself. How could we all come from heavenly worship at vespers and then go to the basement and give each other hell and still get ready for Liturgy tomorrow morning? It was an awful spiritual roller coaster ride and I was thinking I might have made a mistake joining this Orthodox parish. Orthodoxy looked so good in the books.

I walked with my arm around my wife and we went upstairs. We sat on a couple chairs and shared our fears about what kind of faith community we had brought our family into. The Orthodox Church seemed to be falsely advertised by those books I read. Or was this just a little friction in communal Christianity?

Two men, who would later become my friends and one the Godfather to my second daughter were about to leave when they saw us dumbfounded from the meeting.

I asked, "Are all the meetings like that?"

They both looked at me and laughed. One of them said, "Oh that? That was nothing—last year he threw a punch."

Another kind older gentleman behind them coming up the stairs laughed too.

The two left.

"Mr. Ayoub, is that true?"

He smiled and said, "Those two are jokers."

Mr. Ayoub sensed the concern on my face, saw my wife's eyes and sat down next to us.

"How can we come from vespers and then act like that? I don't get it?" I said and dropped my head into my hands.

There was a long pause and then he put his hand on my

back and said in his heavy Arabic accented voice, "Do you come from a large family?"

"Kind of, I mean they are all a lot younger, but yeah, aunts, uncles, cousins, I guess so," I said.

"Do they ever fight?" He asked.

"Of course."

"Do they still love one another?"

"Of course."

"Well, what you don't understand is that not only are we a church family but most people in this parish are related—cousins or in-laws. What you saw was a little family argument, but it all stays down there in the basement. Tomorrow all will be forgiven and we will move on. When you love someone, that's what happens every now and then. It's how we do it. We may fight each other every now and then but we put our arms around each other afterward and move on. We're a family, we love one another," he said with a smile.

"So has anyone ever thrown a punch in a general assembly?"

This man, Nicholas Ayoub, slapped me on the back and laughed. Popped some gum in his mouth, stood up and said, "See you tomorrow, brother."

I went home that night and laid in bed thinking about the words of wisdom shared by Nick Ayoub, a very loving and fatherly figure for us. I thought about how Christ had zealousness for the Temple and flipped over tables and cleansed the

Temple of money changers,[56] the apostle Paul got up in Peter's face in Antioch, of all places, and chewed him out.[57] And of course there was St. Nicholas and Arius. Family must be worth fighting for and with sometimes. Orthodoxy was certainly not an individualistic religion—just me, Jesus, and my Bible.

I was comforted by the thought that I was joining a family and not just a parish. In Protestantism I would have left and started shopping for another Church. There was no turning back for us now. No way out of making good on the wagers I had made with God.

That next Sunday morning, my quarrelsome brothers and sisters in Christ partook of the healing power of the Eucharist. They were sorting through the real issues of the parish at coffee hour. It was as if the Lord had visited the members of our little council like he did St. Nicholas at Nicaea. The priest was talking with those most vocal last night showing a fatherly affection. The friction of last night was replaced with brotherly love, laughing, and embracing one another.

I turned to my wife and asked, "Wow, what happened last night and who are these crazy people?"

She said, "This is what love looks like and these people are family now."

---

[56] "Then Jesus went into the temple of God and drove out all those who bought and sold in the temple, and overturned the tables of the money changers and the seats of those who sold doves" (Matthew 21:12).
[57] "Now when Peter had come to Antioch, I withstood him to his face, because he was to be blamed..." (Galatians 2: 11-21).

r. leo olson

WINEBIBBING IN THE KINGDOM

Christian white men don't know how to dance at a party. It's true. Except for ballroom dancing and maybe some swing dancing, I have no memory of a Christian white man not looking ridiculous while fast dancing. Sure, get some beers in us old Bible thumpers and we can gyrate around but we're a little too stuffy, a little too puritanical in our make-up to ever look good dancing. But the Orthodox know how to throw a party and dance up a storm. It comes from centuries where *fasting* and *feasting* were the cycles of living in an Orthodox agrarian based culture. The seasons and Church feast days were sacred and served as the 'life calendar' instead of sports, political elections and the fall TV line ups governing our modern culture.

Orthodox spirituality has cycles of restricting the governing passions of life to enhance spiritual awareness—eating, entertainment and even when to have sex! These 'fasts' appear strict compared to the instant gratification, all you can eat buffets, and enlarged breasted sexually obsessive culture of America—and they are. Orthodox spirituality has a wonderful quality of combining the physical side and the spiritual side of life. They call it synergy and it is a theologically rich term.

When I was a Protestant I called it, my 'walk with the

Lord' and tended to view it as a 'part' of my life. I had a prayer life, a spiritual life, a work life, a social life, a church involvement life. These 'parts' were viewed slightly different from each other, although I tried to be Christian in all of them. They were life compartments, like boxes I could pull out from the closet and work on. Orthodox spirituality is not dualistic or compartmentalized but combines all these aspects or 'parts' of life—synergy is the best word. It is because of this synergy and lack of compartmentalization that I was always scandalized by the stories of Catholic weddings and judged Orthodox Christians of being 'earthy' which was code for drinking, dancing and swearing too much. They were 'wine-bibbers'.[58]

Fasting is the best example of how this spiritual synergy works. There are more days when an Orthodox Christian is expected to fast from wine, oil, and all animal products than not. There are certain days and periods of times when a married couple is supposed to curb the 'other' appetite.[59] Now we're talking food and sex here, two biggies that have more to do with spirituality than I ever would have guessed.

As soon I would deny myself, die to my passions even a little, a battle started inside of me. By the third day of fasting I'm usually horny and hungry beyond normal. New York strip

---

[58] "The Son of Man came eating and drinking, and they say, 'Look, a glutton and a winebibber, a friend of tax collectors and sinners!' But wisdom is justified by her children" (Matthew 11:19).

[59] "Do not deprive one another except with consent for a time, that you may give yourselves to fasting and prayer; and come together again so that Satan does not tempt you because of your lack of self-control" (I Corinthians 7:5).

goes on sale at an insanely low price. McDonalds brings back the McRib. My wife becomes even more attractive. The physical and spiritual synergy of Orthodox spirituality goes haywire. But this is also my chance to actually work on virtues, like self-control. Fasting periods are usually brutal for me because my personal 'synergy' is lop sided and I've often failed at fasting, (damn that McRib) but I get to learn about humility and dependence on God—more virtues. However, when it's time to break the 'fast' and 'feast'—party hardy. Then a hidden joy that I can't explain in words is experienced and it is dynamically satisfying, joyful, fun and honoring to God.

∞

We were the first of our Protestant friends to join Orthodoxy. Others were still seeking and working through the counter-intuitive forms of worship and the authoritative claims the Orthodox Church made on ones' life and beliefs. Most liked the beauty, mysticism and absolute claims of being the true Church but struggled with unlearning God and leaving the Christian life they were brought up in. Plus, what kind of people were these Orthodox Christians? No one had much exposure to Greeks, Arabs or Russians—lions, tigers and bears, oh my.

The social hesitations were felt by some of the Orthodox families as we were getting to know each other at coffee hours and after speakers at special services. So the idea of a social mixer where several 'seeking' couples were invited to get to know several of the Orthodox families from the parishes in town was arranged.

In Grand Rapids, the priests encourage people who are 'on their way' to Orthodoxy to visit all the parishes in town and choose where to attend. I didn't like this practice but that's because I came from a Christian tradition where 'church shopping' was all too common. If I wasn't being 'fed' by the preaching or the pastor said something that offended me or I didn't like the color of the new carpet, I could leave and shop around for a new church family. But that's what the priest said to do, so Protestant 'seekers' are left with the awful process of how to evaluate a parish. We all shared our experiences and bits of our conversations with each other trying to judge which parish was more 'ethnic' than the others.

It's really an awful process and it feels wrong, like stereotyping people groups, but Orthodoxy was like discovering a spiritual foreign land, and injured people, like me, were wise to navigate it carefully because so much could be misunderstood. It was also good for me to be *wrong* about so many 'Christian' things. I was sick with pride and my sickness infected others by constantly telling people they were wrong based on 'chapter and verse' theology. The more time I spent around these 'winebibbers' the severity of my spiritual head injuries were exposed. I was soul sick. I was a Christian Pharisee. The more I got to know these people the more wrong I was about these people. Humility was the iodine for my sick soul.

A social mixer seemed like a good idea to get to know the people from the parishes. It was a fine gathering. There was much laughter, great food, good wine and a little too much cleavage to be an official church event.

In one conversation this struggle to 'evaluate' a parish was shared and one gentleman with great wisdom and candor told us he would bottom line it for us. The faces in the group lit up. Bottom lining is the Protestant caviar of spiritual wisdom. In Protestantism it's all about the bottom line: 'What does the Bible say about that?' or 'which point of doctrine is going to be the last straw before I leave and church shop?' or the ultimate bottom line—'what does it take to get saved?' Give it to us simple, pure, cold and on an unsalted bland cracker.

Having everyone's complete and undivided attention, several people gripping their drinks with white knuckles, he smiled and spoke this parable, "Orthodoxy in America is like a large boat on the ocean..."

Yes, a nautical parable; I'm a descendant of Vikings,—bring on the lox and caviar.

"...There are two levels to this boat. On the upper level are the Greeks and Arabs and we are partying it up. Life is good in America and we are having a good time on the upper deck dancing away. Down below in the gallows with oars rowing us, fighting the waves and storms are the Russians. We are all on the boat but it seems like for now, anyway, they are doing the hard work. So the question is, who do you want as shipmates?"

We all thought we understood his tongue and cheek parable but we didn't. I was confused even more and wondered if I had chosen the right parish after all. I was a serious Christian, injured but ready to work on my life of healing repentance. I wagered my 'party' life when I was eighteen. I didn't want a Christian 'party' life——that sounded just horrible and no fun at all.

The evening continued and much good had been done to make everyone feel welcomed and wanted by these pretty normal Americanized Orthodox people. There was no overt recruiting just flattery and acknowledgment that we probably understood Orthodoxy better than they did——at least theologically. I knew the theological 'accent' but I didn't know the spiritual language.

As people left the social mixer some whispered invitations of another party coming up called a *hafli*[60] at St. Nicholas. I couldn't find a spiritual or theological definition anywhere about practicing a *hafli*. Hesychasm (mystical inner prayer)—— yes! Hadji (pilgrim to the holy Sepulcher)——yes! Hermitry (solitary and secluded monastic life)——yes! Hafli——no!

∞

Since my wife and I had joined the parish of St. Nicholas, we started to see more hafli announcements in the bulletin.

"Should we go?" I asked my wife.

She replied, "Absolutely!"

She's great, good in social settings, has a great laugh, likes to have a good time, sociable, musical and can dance——exactly the opposite of me. I know I will stand against a wall and analyze everything because, well, I'm a Christian white man and I don't know how to dance.

We walked into the church hall and it was a little too dark,

---

[60] Loosely defined and transliterates in English to 'party'.

the music was a little too loud, and there was a little too much cleavage to be an official church event. Someone handed me two drink tickets. There was strange food everywhere; hummus, olives, triangular bread pies and all kinds of appetizers I didn't recognize and couldn't pronounce. There was a dance floor where a 'conga' line of dancers was snaking around tables and everyone was kicking and stepping in unison. There really was dancing on the upper deck of the Orthodox boat, I thought.

My wife noticed some type of informal lesson off to the side being taught by a woman who was at least seventy but nimble and quick. I noticed our priest was watching the lesson. We rolled up next to him. He smiled at us and said, "Just raise one hand in the air and act like you're twisting out a light bulb and hop around to the rhythm of the drum beat. That's all there is to it." My wife jumped right into the practice lesson.

I left her and assumed my post against the wall. Someone came up to me and tried to get me to join the tribal line dancing. No way in hell I'm going out there, I thought, but smiled and kindly shook my head, 'no'.

I watched from the wall. A guy with a big drum came from somewhere and then the party kicked into high gear. I noticed the priest made an exit when another guy climbed on a table and sang-along in Arabic to his favorite song. There was talk of setting up a hookah but I don't know what came of that. This party was off the hook and I had no idea how this fit into Orthodoxy. The closest thing in my Christian upbringing to compare with this was a spicy chili cook-off at the church picnic. Maybe I should just grab an oar, keep my head down and row.

I was not comfortable so I started to look for an exit when I noticed my wife out on the dance floor. She was laughing, dancing, arm in arm with a Jordanian man and a Palestinian woman. She had the biggest smile on her face that I'd seen in years, maybe even ever.

That's when it hit me—I really am on some kind of spiritual boat packed with others very different from me. We are being saved all together, two by two—arm in arm. The tradition of Christianity I grew up in defined itself by being separate from the worldly things. The people lived in fractured, disconnected spiritual row boats. Forty thousand different denominations all bottom-lined the minimum doctrinal statements for individualized salvation but could not agree on anything else in the Bible. We all held on to the life preservers of our favorite Bible verses and scoffed at the Catholic and Orthodox arks as they passed us by.

Now I was on Noah's ark, sealed with the chrism of the Holy Spirit just as God had sealed the door on Noah's gopher wood ark.[61] There were many different 'animals' on this boat and I was one of them, all wet, still half holding my broken life preserver. I was being saved together with all the beautiful

---

[61] Blessed water and olive oil are used in the sacraments of Baptism and Chrismation. The flood account of Genesis 7 is referenced in the prayers as the arch-type for these sacraments. The ark is the Orthodox Church. The flood is obviously a type of baptism. Baptized Christians not in communion with the Orthodox Church, who want to join, do so by the sacrament of Chrismation—anointing with holy oil. God sent a dove with an olive twig to tell creation that is was safe and new life awaited them.

creatures of God whose inner fasting had broken and now it was time to feast and enjoy the gifts of food, wine and fellowship which restored the joy of salvation in us all.[62] I was wonderfully scandalized by it all.

I knew there certainly was work to be done on this boat but there was dancing to be done on the boat as well. Orthodox Christianity was infused, ingrained, woven together through several different cultures; Greek, Arab, Russian, Romanian, Albanian and now it was crashing into the head waters of the Protestant American culture. It sure looked strange but it was good medicine for a fractured schizophrenic soul to see people living a faith that was inclusive of all aspects of life and still had fun.

That was exactly what I witnessed at the hafli, a fully integrated expression of Christianity mixed into every aspect of a culture. This multi-ethnic, multi-generational, trans-historical, cosmically connected Christian community redeemed time from the profane to the sacred by fasting and feasting. They consumed real food for enjoyment and real spiritual food for nutrition;[63] prayed ancient corporate prayers and private inner prayers; repented and celebrated; cried and laughed; lived and died all as a unified body of believers. This

---

[62] "He causes the grass to grow for the cattle, and vegetation for the service of man, that he may bring forth food from the earth, And wine *that* makes glad the heart of man, oil to make *his* face shine, and bread which strengthens man's heart" (Psalm 104:14-15).

[63] "Most assuredly, I say to you, unless you eat the flesh of the Son of Man and drink His blood, you have no life in you. Whoever eats My flesh and drinks My blood has eternal life, and I will raise him up at the last day. For My flesh is food indeed, and My blood is drink indeed..." (John 6:53-55).

was and is an extension of the true early Church, where Christ is above all things and is in all and fills all things—ALL things.[64]

There was a time to party in an authentic Christian life and this was a type of spiritual electroshock therapy for my spiritual head injuries. I had been so consumed with the gout of my private, individual, cerebral-spiritual life, from the childish doubts that I may not escape hell-fire and the constant guilt and fear of the dooms-day second coming of Christ that I forgot how to have fun and experience the times of joy in this Christian life. I was filled with such happiness watching my wife dance and laugh and party. I would have joined her in the hafli line-dance but I'm a white Christian man and I can't dance. Just hand me an oar until I am better healed.

---

[64] "He who descended is also the One who ascended far above all the heavens, that He might fill all things" (Ephesians 4:10).

I AM A C. I AM A C-O

I am a C
I am a C-H
I am a C-H-R-I-S-T-I-A-N
And I have C-H-R-I-S-T
In my H-E-A-R-T
And I will L-I-V-E E-T-E-R-N-A-L-L-Y

These are the words to a Protestant Sunday school song. Go to anybody raised in a Protestant tradition and repeat these lyrics and I will bet you ten push-ups that they will know this song and sing it for you. If you are lucky enough to have multiple Protestants in this discussion they may even sing it in rounds for you.

One of my friends at St. Nicholas has often made fun of us 'converts' to Orthodoxy. In Orthodoxy if you are from Western European descent and were raised as a Protestant and joined Orthodoxy you are forever referred to as a 'convert'. Conversely if you are of Greek, Russian, Arab, Egyptian, African, or Eastern European descent and were born into Orthodoxy then you are referred to as a 'cradle' Orthodox. For now it's a friendly labeling system until my children, who are 'cradle' and American grow up.

After the Divine Liturgy this friend asked me why I only went to one knee, like a football player, when everyone else was kneeling with both knees. I smiled knowing that he was teasing me, and then he held his hand in the shape of a 'C' to his forehead and started to sing:

I am a C

I am a C-O

I am a C-O-N-V-E-R-T...

Everyone within ear shot laughed.

It's a playful Orthodox inside joke when a 'cradle Orthodox' points out a small 't' tradition done oddly by a 'convert'. Being raised in a non-liturgical tradition I sometimes improvise the Orthodox liturgical calisthenics, like crossing yourself, kissing an icon, bowing, kneeling, full prostrations and when to cross yourself.

Now I can take a joke and a little teasing but I must confess that something has always pricked at my heart when I'm labeled a 'convert'. I mean, I grew up in a Christian home, I have a Christian higher education degree, I even went to seminary. I have always thought of myself as a Christian even before joining Orthodoxy—maybe not a particularly good one but why the label?

The label of 'convert' has a second class feel to it. Oh, no one will admit that, and I don't believe that is true, but it has that sting or stigma to it sometimes. The 'convert' label had laid scabbed over in my heart for years but for some reason it was picked open and bled a spirit of contention in me.

I now took offense at being labeled a 'convert'. It also confused me as to how I should view other Christian faith traditions, and whether I would ever be considered a full member of the Orthodox family or just a spiritual step-child. I thought I unlearned using a code of conduct as a spiritual measuring stick and I didn't like to be patted on the head and told I was worshiping God wrong. I know this type of behavior policing and it stirred bad memories for me—stuff I was trying to unlearn and be healed from.

So I decided to go to my 'spiritual father'[65] and tell him my pains which could very well be coming from my spiritual head injuries. My spiritual father is a good soul doctor who often prescribes tasks of obedience to bring about repentance. He knows my brand of Protestantism and is very gentle with me spiritually—like a real live visible guardian angel.

We sat down for coffee one day and I blurted out, "I don't like being made fun of for the way I worship. I mean who cares if I do something different. For God's sake, I'm still learning this stuff. There is a bigger learning curve for Baptists anyway, right? Oh and I don't like to be called a 'convert'. It's not like I was a Muslim or a Jew or a Mormon. I've been 'reconciled' to the historic Church. Am I some kind of a second class Christian or something? The whole label thing is starting to piss me off, so Father, I would prefer the label, 'reconciled' to 'convert'."

---

[65] In Orthodoxy a 'spiritual father' is someone who you confess your sins to and commit to obey his spiritual instructions. The primary goal is to help you along the way of salvation and to teach you to repent. They get to look into your soul and be God's instrument for healing. It can be your local priest or a monastic. It can even be a holy layperson, man or woman, they just cannot perform sacrament of absolution.

I had wagered everything with God many times in my life so I tend to lay it out there kind of raw with my spiritual father. I figured doctors need to know the extent of the injuries in order to help you. Plus I liked to make the most of my time with ministering 'angels' when I get the chance.

He listened, looked at the floor and spun his prayer rope. I know he was trying to focus his mind on prayer, probably, the Jesus Prayer,[66] so as to not just give his own opinion. It soon created an awkward silence, and just like the lawyer who wanted to justify himself by asking Jesus, 'who his neighbor was?'[67] I broke the silence and asked, "Am I right to feel this way about the 'convert' label thing?"

He looked at me as only he does and said, "No. That's just your pride muddying your thoughts. We are all converts." And that was it.

He is a man of few words, always gentle but straight forward in his advice of which I shamefully test and try before I can admit he's right. People injured with pride and spiritual authority issues, like me, do this. Our conversation switched to another topic. He didn't fix me, that's not his job, but he opened the door in my soul where the One who does fix me started to work.

I felt the same way about the whole label thing for several months after our meeting and thought it wise to voice my

---

[66] A special prayer continuously repeated in silence to quiet the mind and bring the presence of God. 'Lord Jesus Christ, son of God, have mercy upon me, a sinner.'

[67] "But he, wanting to justify himself, said to Jesus, "And who is my neighbor?" (Luke 10:29).

spirit of contention to my other so-called 'convert' friends. That proved to be not very wise at all and another source for more chiding from 'cradles'. It was my hang up, my pride, and I let it stew in my soul.

∞

On the feast day of Pentecost[68] the sacred duty of preaching the Word of God for eight to twelve minutes fell to one of our gracious deacons—a wonderful homeliest in his own right but not immune to my mental drifting during sermons. My spiritual head injuries often prevent me from listening to sermons. I usually get a spiritual cramp or experience a flashback to some type of guilt riddled spiritually manipulating sermon of my past. On good days I daydream but on bad days I pull out my concealed weapon and unfairly critique the hell out of the sermon. I had no weapon pulled because this deacon was a humble and virtuous man and it was a good day for me.

The homily started out with the familiar 'birthday of the Church' theme and referenced the Epistle reading from the book of Acts chapter two. He pointed to the twelve foot icon of the feast of Pentecost in our parish, and then said something that sent me off on a day-dream.

I remember it this way: "Our Lord, the incarnate Second Person of the Trinity is recorded in history. There are eye-

---

[68] This feast in Acts 2 describes how Jesus formed the one holy catholic and apostolic Church and the promised coming of the Holy Spirit that would lead the Church in all truth.

witnesses to His ministry. They were revealed in actual historical events of the past. His birth by the Theotokos, His baptism by His cousin St. John, His ministry of miracles and healings by thousands, His Death, Burial, Descent into Hades, Resurrection and Ascension by hundreds of witnesses.[69] His whole life was grounded in human history—in the past. However, now is the 'Age of the Holy Spirit' and that allows us to participate in these events today. The Holy Spirit, the giver of life..." He went on.

I thought about how amazing miracles during the feast of Pentecost described in the book of Acts must have been. I wished I was there, seeing miracles, visions, healings by the mere shadows of the apostles passing over the lame![70] The Holy Spirit enabled simple unlearned fishermen to explain the gospel in several different languages at once. I thought how funny it must have been to accuse the Apostles of being drunk as the Holy Spirit converted over three thousand in one sermon to the infant Church.[71]

---

[69] "Then, behold, the veil of the temple was torn in two from top to bottom; and the earth quaked, and the rocks were split, and the graves were opened; and many bodies of the saints who had fallen asleep were raised; and coming out of the graves after His resurrection, they went into the holy city and appeared to many" (Matthew 27:51-53).

[70] "And believers were increasingly added to the Lord, multitudes of both men and women, so that they brought the sick out into the streets and laid *them* on beds and couches, that at least the shadow of Peter passing by might fall on some of them" (Acts 5:14-16).

[71] "Then they were all amazed and marveled, saying to one another, "Look, are not all these who speak Galileans? And how is it that we hear, each in our own language in which we were born? Parthians and Medes and Elamites, those dwelling in Mesopotamia, Judea and Cappadocia,

The Holy Spirit worked obviously and convincingly through diverse miracles. The infant Church created instant converts, real converts—now that would have been something to see. Sure they were accused of being drunk in the Spirit and doing crazy things but everyone was a 'convert', both Jew and Gentile, priests and pagans, soldiers and senators.

I wondered why we don't see miracles like those today. I could go home and flip on the cable Christian television shows and see 'miracles' but I'm too skeptical of the sensationalism and profit margin of it all—instant skepticism is one of my spiritual head injuries.

It seemed to me that the miracles, in the 'Age of the Holy Spirit' as our good deacon was preaching about, would obviously and convincingly produce converts to the Church— that's what the Holy Spirit does. The Orthodox Church has an occasional miraculous weeping icon that usually scares the priests and laity into repentance. There are boasts of holy relics performing miracles but they do not typically produce mass converts, just mass media coverage or mass pilgrim foot traffic.

Pontus and Asia, Phrygia and Pamphylia, Egypt and the parts of Libya adjoining Cyrene, visitors from Rome, both Jews and proselytes, Cretans and Arabs—we hear them speaking in our own tongues the wonderful works of God." So they were all amazed and perplexed, saying to one another, "Whatever could this mean?" But Peter, standing up with the eleven, raised his voice and said to them, "Men of Judea and all who dwell in Jerusalem, let this be known to you, and heed my words. For these are not drunk, as you suppose, since it is only the third hour of the day" (Acts 2:7-15).

Then the words of my spiritual father echoed in my mind. I looked over at the rest of our parish, a cosmopolitan of ethnic families; Lebanese, Palestinian, Jordanian, Eritrean, German, English, Scandinavian, Polish and Dutch all listening to an Arabic descended deacon preach the Word of God in a language that we all understood—calling us all to repent and convert our lives back to Christ. It was a little Pentecost. The work of the Holy Spirit started back on the original feast day of Christian Pentecost and is an ongoing spiritual reality happening this very day. My spiritual father was right, again—we are all converts.

In Orthodoxy, part of my healing process was to realize that daily, I needed to repent and transform my perspective of life from just centering around my physical needs and my spiritual interests to a life centered on God's love for others, living in His Kingdom and being busy about His work. I must intentionally and often re-dress the wounds of my spiritual head injuries with the healing sacramental bandages. I must convert myself daily to live life on this earth, as best as I can, deciphering in this modern culture how Jesus and his band of followers would have.

It didn't matter anymore if I was labeled a 'convert'. I now understood that the Holy Spirit is always mystically and authentically converting us all! The Comforter is constantly converting us from death to life with every Eucharistic meal we eat; breathing new life into us with every prayer we whisper; forgiving us at every confession as we dry our eyes, and illuminating our souls with every candle we light.

Our deacon was almost done with his homily and my

eyes were opened to the true miracle of Pentecost: The heavenly King, the Comforter, the Spirit of Truth, who is in all places and fills all things, has come to dwell in us, with us, among us just as real as the Lord Jesus Christ did among the disciples. Through the historic Orthodox Church He is calling all people to unity in a new life of spiritual solidarity. A call to miraculously 'convert' a people who love each other, forgive and heal one another and yes, every now and then laugh at a misstep in the Orthodox calisthenics of veneration and worship.

I am a convert to Christ with spiritual head injuries. Every now and then I may look like I'm drunk in the spirit and play around a little bit in the Kingdom of God but at least I'm in the right place when the Holy Spirit is pouring out His healing love. As long as I remain in humility and make sincere efforts to connect with the Divine, then I can be assured of a full recovery of spiritual head injuries…someday.

r. leo olson

WHAT LANGUAGE IS THIS?

Part of unlearning God and the recovery process for my spiritual head injuries has been to figure out how to talk about an Orthodox understanding of God, her different spirituality and sometimes the ethnocentric life within her. How could I describe what I was experiencing and then tell others without shredding the spirituality of the people from my past? I thought rather than try to explain everything, maybe I should invite them to come and see for themselves. It worked for me.

The first couple of times I invited some of my Protestant friends and family, the service was not entirely in English—a little Greek or Arabic was explainable and acceptable. When a real live bishop was coming to visit, I broke out the first century letters from St. Ignatius and boasted about how the mystical and true Church manifests itself in a special way when the bishop is present. Some of my seeker friends were excited about this and decided to come and visit.

Of course, the bishop chose to chant in Arabic almost the entire service. I was defeated. I was experiencing a real, incarnational relationship with God and yet could not explain to others why whole parts of the Divine Liturgy were in a different language. I wanted Orthodoxy to be the faith tradition for them, where they could find meaning, healing and encounter God in a real 'come and see' for yourself kind of way. Which language was spoken became a real issue for me as it does for most Protestant seekers and seasoned converts.

I felt like such an American elitist when I demanded the services be entirely in English from my priest. I told him I knew I needed to embrace Orthodox spirituality and worship but could not, would not, if I had to learn Arabic, Russian or Greek. *I'm an American for God's sake, why do I need to learn a new language?* My spiritual head injuries had flared up again.

I had invited some of my siblings to come to a Christmas Eve service. My brothers and sisters are quite a bit younger than me and for the most part are products of a mixed Pentecostal/Baptist Christian tradition. Most of them were working through their own 'unlearning' of God but had not engaged their faith seriously since they left the practices and faith communities of their own childhoods.

They knew I had moved to a different church and were suspicious that it was a totally different religion. So what better way to show them original Christianity than to invite them to an Orthodox service before a Christmas family party? I mean Christmas is about the birth of Jesus and who He was and why He was born—to save us. I thought if I could start with that fundamental truth then that would serve as a foundation for other conversations with them.

We met at my house before the service because I wanted to prepare them, pre-proselytize them, if you will. I had an arsenal of articles, magic Gillquist pamphlets and timelines of church history. I talked for an hour. I was eloquent. I was smooth. I was channeling St. John Chrysostom.[72]

This turned out to be a horrible idea, grossly misjudged by me. I anticipated some of the normal questions about 'high church' liturgics, chanting, icons and why St. George is slaying a dinosaur like a dungeon and dragons character. I even tackled the 'venerational' kissing of icons as not idolatry. I told them it's like kissing a picture of Grandma who had Jesus in her heart and there-by reverencing the work of the Holy Spirit not worshipping Kodak. I could tell I was speaking a foreign language to them and they suspected spiritual trickery of me.

We caravanned to the service. I knew my brother did not want to go to my church because he did not listen to my pre-emptive lecture trying desperately to translate Orthodoxy into his world. But he was forced to attend due to family pressure. We all stood in the back pew of the darkened nave and my brother sat down after one psalm was read, put his hat on and pulled it down low over his eyes. He had checked out seven minutes into the service. The rest of my siblings were

---

[72] St. John Chrysostom (347-407 AD) was known for his eloquence in preaching and public speaking, and assembling the *Divine Liturgy of St. John Chrysostom*. He was given the Greek epithet *chrysostomos*, meaning "golden mouthed".

wide-eyed, confused and feeling self-conscience that they
were under-dressed.

An older gentleman from our parish made his way over to
us from the very front and asked my brother to take off his
hat. This experience was so horrible for me, I went inside my
head and silently recited 'Lord have mercy' over and over as
fast as I could to get away from my embarrassment.

My brother did take off his hat but did not stand up. He
folded his arms with verve and his stubbornness set in. I knew
he would endure this Orthodox service once but never again.
I recognized this inner passive revolt because we have the
same spiritual head injuries. I also knew it was hopeless to try
and fix this but I leaned down to him anyway and half apolo-
gizing and half wanting to punch him in the neck for acting
like a jerk asked, "So pretty different, hey? What do you think
so far?"

He looked up at me and asked, "What language is this?"

I couldn't help but laugh and answered, "Um, it's English.
The whole thing has been in English so far."

He rolled his eyes and waited the service out. There was
'no room at the Inn' for my brother and I'm pretty sure he
wouldn't have stayed at 'hotel Orthodoxy' if a room was
offered. He has never been back and we have not discussed
Orthodoxy or God since.

∞

We had a priest who was born in Syria. He spoke English
very well, a slight accent but definitely bi-lingual, probably

still dreamt in Arabic. Our family loved him even though his stay was brief at our parish.

Sometimes during the Divine Liturgy he would read the priestly prayers in Arabic. These prayers are supposed to be silent, according to the red service book in the pew, but most priests say them quietly. It's a fun 'cultural' experience to try and follow along as Arabic is being read by the priest right to left and in the book it's written left to right in English. However, on this particular Sunday morning, it was more than just the 'silent' prayers of the priest; he was going off in Arabic, almost the whole service. My wife could tell bees were buzzing around my head during the service about this issue.

Soon after joining this ancient and sacred tradition of worship I was able to formulate my own sinful nit-pickings. It happens to everyone. We all have those mole hills that we make mountains out of from time to time. Arabic dominating the services was mine. I was in desperate need of healing and my whole inner life revolved around learning Orthodox worship not language lessons.

Over half way through the Divine Liturgy our priest was still not using English. I leaned forward and asked a woman in front of us, of Palestinian descent, "What is he saying?"

This was very bad of me. I knew there was no good to come from asking this. As an immigrant she didn't catch the frustrated American sarcasm of my spiritual head injuries coming out—thank God. But my wife knew full well where my heart was and I could feel her stare in the back of my head.

The woman, leaned back and said, "I don't know. I can't understand his accent."

I laughed through my nose and leaned back. My wife looked at me with eyes that said, 'I had crossed the line'. I whispered to her, "Even she doesn't know what the hell language this is."

Her eyes steeled and she replied, "You've got a problem and you should watch your own language before you critique the priest."

Afterward, I spoke to the priest about his 'over' use of Arabic in the service. I told him I come here to worship and Arabic is a problem for me. I don't know what you are saying up there. I could tell he sensed a spiritual head injury in my tone.

"Habibi,[73] was God praised and glorified today even if you didn't know the words?" He asked.

He smiled at me without another word of correction needed. I smiled back, full of inner shame that I let my spiritual head injuries lash out like that.

∞

Flashback a few years when my wife and I wanted to visit every parish in town before choosing one to join—that horrible predicament for converts; we had to judge parishes by our own likes and dislikes. We had all but decided to join St. Nicholas but there was one more parish in town we hadn't visited. So we did.

---

[73] 'Loved one' in Arabic.

Fr. John Estephan, may he rest in peace, was the priest. Fr. John was a highly educated man. He held two doctorates, one in the history of the Middle East and the other in anthropology. He was an ambassador to Lebanon from Mexico, spoke five different languages, of which English was his last and least fluent. He was a priest that served our city for decades and when he fell asleep in the Lord a couple years ago, the true fruits of his ministry were seen by all.

However, as I said, English was the last of his languages and he spoke with a thick accent. The Liturgy was great and the choir was grand. Orthodox worship with its ancient ritual and minor toned chanting often transports everyone to a mystical manifestation of the Kingdom of God. I was raptured in spiritual revelry. Then came the homily.

Fr. John walked slowly to the podium with many notes and started preaching in English for the most part. He would explain something in Arabic and then in English. It was like he was the speaker and translator for his own sermon. Towards the end of the sermon, he pounded his fist into the podium and said, "If you are not grateful—you are not Christian! How can you say you love someone and not be grateful to them."

That was all I needed to hear or understand from Fr. John Estephan. We did not choose St. George as a parish because of the 'language issue' on our horrible parish evaluation list of 'likes and dislikes'. However, to this day, many years later, I have not forgotten the simple truth of those twenty-two words from Fr. John.

∞

St. Paul wrote in First Corinthians 13—the 'love chapter' quoted in almost every marriage ceremony: "Though I speak with the tongues of men and of angels, but have not love, I have become sounding brass or a clanging cymbal" (I Corinthians 13:1).

I was the one spiritually injured with the 'language issue' not Orthodoxy. Truth transcends language. Orthodox worship engages all the faculties and senses of a person: touch, taste, smell, feel, hearing, mind, and soul.

My spiritual head injuries deformed my idea of worship because it was hyper-cerebral and still self-centered. If I didn't understand the language then it was of no use to me. I demanded Orthodoxy conform to me and my American way of thinking rather than let it transform me through the universal language of God—love. I had become a 'clanging symbol' to those around me by pridefully demanding English only.

The shining light of truth and the healing spiritual medicine of love, known in Orthodoxy, made its way to the 'land of the free and the home of the brave' not by religious crusade or rational enlightenment movements but by way of immigrants. Many risked their own lives and forsook all they owned, their loved ones, and all they knew about life to come here to America. They brought with them the most ancient expression of Christianity and worshipped in spirit and in truth the only way they knew how and in the language they spoke. Who was I to demand the terms and conditions of

God's blessings of Orthodox worship? I had a Jonah complex and that didn't work out so good for Jonah when he didn't agree with God about the Ninevites.[74]

I don't know how many times I've said, "I wish I knew another language?" Well, I can sample Arabic and Greek and Russian anytime I want. And unlike my years of studying swear words in French and Spanish classes, I get to learn the very best words in those languages and sing 'Lord have mercy' or shout 'Christ is risen!" at Easter in multiple languages. To learn the words of praise to our Lord in another language is a great privilege. I am grateful for different languages now. Healing from spiritual head injuries requires the closing of a myopic eye and an open-hearted grateful embrace towards someone else and sometimes an entire culture. Orthodoxy is here in America but it is wrapped in a cultural wrapping paper like a Christmas present.

When I reflect on the 'language issue' now, I remember when my brother didn't even recognize English in that Christmas Eve service. I spoke so many words to him before he visited. I made biblical assassin arguments about how the Church came before the Bible. I used hollow point long range bullets to shoot down praise bands and 'pep rally' worship. I said this...bang! I said that...fire in the hole! I, I, I and none

---

[74] Jonah was the reluctant prophet of God. He did not want to share God's message with a foreign people. After being swallowed by a fish and vomited on a beach, he angrily preached God's message then went on a hill to watch the Ninevites burn. They repented. Jonah was consumed with anger at God's mercy on a foreign people. He was even pissed at God about the shade plant that died no longer providing him shade while he hoped for Nineveh's destruction. (Ref. Jonah 4)

of it mattered because there was no love in my words, no gratefulness. He heard only clanging symbols on that Christmas Eve.

When I am truly grateful for the Lord's gift of Orthodoxy, instead of demanding He tell me He loves me in English only, my cold Jonah-like heart warms. I begin to truly love other people and all their customs, values and even their languages. I begin to heal.

Twenty-two words from Fr. John would have saved me years of frustration and aided my spiritual therapeutic needs; if only I would have had ears to hear then. I would rather say seven true words of faith, hope and love in any language than thousands of my own words that don't mean anything in the end.

At Pascha, (Easter) every patriarch, bishop and priest stands in front of the holy altar of God and proclaims to all, 'Christ is risen!'—the only hope of healing for people with spiritual head injuries and salvation for humankind. The people from around the world shout back, 'Truly He is risen!' And I am among them. What else is there to know, understand or believe?

Jesus Christ, love incarnate, conquered sin, death and hades for all people no matter where they were born or what language they spoke. It is with gratefulness that I stand every Pascha with Orthodox Christians worldwide and mystically with every Christian since the myrrh-bearing women at the tomb discovered it empty, and shout the greatest cosmic archetype mystery of faith, hope and love that the universe has ever heard:

English: Christ is Risen! Truly He is Risen!

Albanian: Krishti U Ngjall! Vertet U Ngjall!
Aleut: Khristus anahgrecum!Alhecum anahgrecum!
Alutuq: Khris-tusaq ung-uixtuq! Pijiinuq ung-uixtuq!
Amharic: Kristos tenestwal! Bergit tenestwal!
Anglo-Saxon: Crist aras! Crist sodhlice aras!
Arabic: L'Messieh kahm! Hakken kahm!
Armenian: Kristos haryav ee merelotz!Orhnial eh harootyunuh
kristosee!
Aroman: Hristolu unghia! Daleehira unghia!
Athabascan: Xristosi banuytashtch'ey!Gheli banuytashtch'ey!
Bulgarian: Hristos voskrese! Vo istina voskrese!
Byelorussian: Khristos uvoskros!Zaprowdu uvoskros!
Chinese: Helisituosi fuhuole!Queshi fuhuole!
or (Cantonese): Gaydolk folkwoot leew! Ta koksut folkwoot leew!
or (Mandarin): Ji-du fu-huo-le!Zhen-de Ta fu-huo-le!
Coptic: Pi-ekhristos Aftonf! Khen oomethmi Aftonf!
Czech: Kristus vstal a mrtvych!Opravdi vstoupil!
Danish: Kristus er opstanden!Kristus er opstanden!
Dutch: Christus is opgestaan! Ja, hij is waarlijk opgestaan!
Eritrean-Tigre: Christos tensiou!Bahake tensiou!
Esperanto: Kristo levigis! Vere levigis!
Estonian: Kristus on oolestoosunt!Toayestee on oolestoosunt!
Ethiopian: Christos t'ensah em' muhtan!Exai' ab-her eokala!
Finnish: Kristus nousi kuolleista!Totistesti nousi!
French: Le Christ est réssuscité! En verite il est réssuscité!
Gaelic: Kriost eirgim! Eirgim!
Georgian: Kriste ahzdkhah!Chezdmaridet!
German: Christus ist erstanden! Er ist wahrhaftig erstanden!
Greek: Christos anesti! Alithos anesti!
Hawaiian: Ua ala hou `o Kristo! Ua ala `I `o no `oia!
Hebrew: Ha Masheeha houh kam! A ken kam! (or Be emet quam!)
Icelandic: Kristur er upprisinn! Hann er vissulega upprisinn!
Indonesian: Kristus telah bangkit!Benar dia telah bangkit!

Italian: Cristo e' risorto! Veramente e' risorto!

Japanese: Harisutosu siochatsu!Makoto-ni siochatsu!

Javanese: Kristus sampun wungu!Saesto panjene ganipun sampun wungu!

Korean: Kristo gesso! Buhar ha sho nay!

Latin: Christus resurrexit! Vere resurrexit!

Latvian: Kristus ir augsham sales!Teyasham ir augsham sales vinsch!

Lugandan: Kristo ajukkide! Amajim ajukkide!Malayalam (Indian): Christu uyirthezhunnettu!Theerchayayum uyirthezhunnettu!

Nigerian: Jesu Kristi ebiliwo! Eziao' biliwo!

Norwegian: Kristus er oppstanden! Han er sannelig oppstanden!

Polish: Khristus zmartvikstau!Zaiste zmartvikstau!

Portugese: Cristo ressuscitou! Em verdade ressuscitou!

Romanian: Hristos a inviat!Adevarat a inviat!

Russian: Khristos voskrese!Voistinu voskrese!

Sanskrit: Kristo'pastitaha! Satvam upastitaha!

Serbian: Cristos vaskres! Vaistinu vaskres!

Slovak: Kristus vstal zmr'tvych!Skutoc ne vstal!

Spanish: Cristos ha resucitado! En verdad ha resucitado!

Swahili: Kristo amefufukka! Kweli Amefufukka!

Swedish: Christus ar uppstanden!Han ar verkligen uppstanden!

Syriac: M'shee ho dkom! Ha koo qam!

Tlingit: Xristos Kuxwoo-digoot!Xegaa-kux Kuxwoo-digoot!

Turkish: Hristos diril-di! Hakikaten diril-di!

Ugandan: Kristo ajukkide! Kweli ajukkide!

Ukranian: Khristos voskres!Voistinu voskres!

Welsh: Atgyfododd Crist!Atgyfododd in wir!

Yupik: Xristusaq Unguixtuq!Iluumun Ung-uixtuq!

Zulu: Ukristu uvukile! Uvukile kuphela!

MY FAILED REFORMATION

Protestants get a bad rap when they join Orthodoxy. The bad rap is that many Orthodox Christians think that when any active Protestant with ministry experience of any kind joins the parish they are equipped to serve in an Orthodox parish ministry because it's the 'same game just a different name'. I have been told many times that I was somehow a better Christian than they were because I was biblically knowledgeable, went to seminary, and presumed to know *how* to do everything church related. 'Just do what you used to do, and bring some of that energy those churches have with you when you were Protestant' has been the proverbial encouragement.

Protestants do seem to be doing something right with the myriads of church programs, institutions and a whole subculture of social, political and corporate networks ingrained in the American culture. But that's because they have home field advantage. America is generally a Protestant Christian nation.

It was formed by many groups of Protestants and some ambiguous deists—it wasn't a bunch of Catholics or Orthodox that signed the Declaration of Independence.[75] So

---

[75] Among the 56 signers of the Declaration of Independence, Charles Carroll was of the four Maryland representatives. He did not sign the Declaration but was excluded as an official delegate because of his faith. He was Catholic.

naturally America has taken on a Protestant flavor in her personality and has set the rules for cultural engagement and assimilation of Orthodoxy into the American melting pot.

American Protestant spirituality and the American culture have many similarities. One of the defining characteristics of Protestant spirituality is being a part of a group of like-minded rugged theological individuals. They define themselves over against other Protestant Christian traditions, Catholicism and Orthodoxy—much like political parties or southern and northern states do.

The Bible is interpreted differently with many conflicting opinions by several different manifestations of Protestants and denominations. Similarly, every four years a political debate takes place between many factions about the Constitution and it's an authoritative claim on all Americans. No one agrees on how to apply it.

A unifying belief of understanding the church as an invisible unified reality[76] on a mission to bring its version of Christianity to the lost world is like the foreign policy of democratic nation building.

And choosing Jesus as a personal and individual savior by way of mental beliefs and special spiritual knowledge from the Bible is like a political independent voting for a presidential

---

[76] Although there is strong theological or biblical interpretative disunity in Protestantism, most hold to a concept of unity realized in the concept of an 'invisible church'—made up of those who have been truly 'saved' by way of special beliefs or prayer rituals, private biblical interpretative knowledge and or ecstatic experiences—a concept which has its roots in a condemned heresy called Nestorianism.

candidate who offers an agreeable governing perspective and promises a better life.

The parallels have made me question whether being an American is its own unique religion modeled after Protestant Christianity. Maybe it's the other way around. The resemblances are problematic for me.

The 'same game different name' bad rap was profoundly obvious to me because Protestantism produced a certain flavor of spirituality that was different than the spirituality I saw in Orthodoxy. Orthodox spirituality is fundamentally different in her organization and life compared to American Protestant spirituality.

I was involved in Protestant gatherings where thousands of people gathered on any given Sunday morning to sing the newest worship songs on a jumbo projector screen and with a full praise band. The children were sent away to have 'little church' while the adults were spiritually fed by either a small group Bible discussion or listened to a thirty to forty minute life-relevant sermon, all the while sipping on a latte during the service. You are the consumer of a brand and the final authority of whether you agree with the brand or not. Protestant church services are user friendly, seeker friendly and have great advertising.

Orthodox spiritually is fundamentally the opposite. Authority rests in the Triune God who established a historical institution that was a spiritual and physical hybrid community called the *Ecclesia* or Church.[77] It acts in collegial fashion with other apostolically succeeded bishops[78] and by extension through formally ordained priests. This living and dynamic authority exercises itself in complete congruity with the Bible as it has been interpreted by everyone everywhere throughout history, the seven Ecumenical Councils with their Church canons, the teachings of sainted 'church fathers', the sacraments, the prayers and services of the faithful. To be in communion with this divine/human, seen/unseen, human/angelic manifestation of the Christian life requires submission and humble obedience to this loving and healing cosmic spiritual communalism. No spiritual cowboys allowed.

Orthodox gatherings involve total fasting from food and water from at least midnight the night before until coffee hour after the Divine Liturgy. We are required to physically participate in worship. We stand for long periods of time and kneel on hard floors. It is very difficult to fall asleep in Orthodox services. Ancient songs are chanted at us in Byzantine tones. The sermon is short and usually not socially topical, while our noisy, crying, naughty little cherubs sit

---

[77] The Greek word ecclesia or church is used by all branches of Christianity but has different meanings. Orthodox and Catholic use the word to mean the historical institution governed hierarchically by a college of bishops around the world. Protestants use the word to describe a spectrum of assemblies or congregations gathered to worship Jesus at God, or even where two or three are gathered in Jesus's name. (Matt. 18:20)

[78] The Orthodox view the pope as the bishop of Rome—a first among equals. There are several bishops which are to lead the Church together, conciliary, like the Apostles of old.

right next to us. We are physically and mystically fed by the awesome and life giving sacraments of the Body and Blood of Christ from a man robed in gold holding a spoon. Orthodox services are not user friendly or seeker friendly with closed communion.[79] They also traditionally have bad advertising compared to American cultural practices.

Even with my spiritual head injuries I recognized this fundamental difference. There was a different type of spirituality being formed here. It was not the 'same game different name' but this 'bad rap' came upon me in full force none the less.

Just over one year after my wife and I joined the Orthodox Church I illustrated this 'bad rap' and almost blew up the Sunday school model as only a good biblical assassin could do. The new priest to our parish was having a hard go of it finding

---

[79] Closed communion means that Orthodox Churches only give communion to other Orthodox Christians who have not separated themselves from the Orthodox community by serious sin or prolonged absence. They must confess a unified belief about God based on the Nicene Creed and submit to the authority of a canonically apostolically succeed bishop. This is motivated by protecting the unity and purity of the Christian faith preserved throughout history by the Orthodox Church. Since the Roman Catholic Church separated from the rest of the Eastern Orthodox regional Churches in 1054, changing the Nicene Creed and claiming sole authority over every other bishop in the world, and every Protestant church broke from the Roman Catholic Church in 1517 with the Reformation the Orthodox will not commune Catholic or Protestant Christians—no unity of belief and no historically verifiable apostolic connection. (It's more complicated with the Catholics and deserves more than a summary footnote but unity of the two historic Churches is on the mend but not a reality yet.)

someone to run the Sunday school ministry, also called church school because it's modeled after American grade schools.

Our priest called us into his office on a weekday and wanted to ask us a favor in person. Being the new 'convert' couple we wanted to please the priest. We were so thankful for just being invited to join Orthodoxy and now the priest needed a favor. We were all smiles as we sat across from him in his office.

He had an infectious smile, laugh and a joyous way about him—his whole demeanor put you in a good mood. He said, "I want you to be the Church school superintendents."

Our smiles turned immediately to grimaces of horror. I was the first to voice our concern—a classic passive aggressive dodge—and said, "Our son is a year old—we'll volunteer as teachers when he is ready to go."

Our priest's smile and enthusiasm were undaunted. "No, habibi's I need you to run the Church school this August."

I looked to my wife and she looked back with the telekinetic connection that married people have and 'told me'—I can't do this. So if you accept, it's all on you.

"Father, you know we support you but this is too much for us. We are so new to the parish and we don't know how to be Orthodox. We..."

"Listen to me. There is a situation that I can't go into. I need to have someone to step in, who has experience in church youth groups. You'll do a good job."

I could tell he was unmoved by our hesitation and I started to question his wisdom. Do you not know that I have spiritual head injuries? You don't know what I could do.

"Father, if you're *asking* us to help you then we have to sadly and humbly decline. We're not ready to lead teachers. We don't know enough to teach the kids in the faith. We should be going to church school classes ourselves—to learn how to raise our son in Orthodoxy."

He smiled at us and remained silent.

"But if you are *telling* us; ordering us as our priest; we will obey you," I said and glanced at my wife for approval at my tactical dodge. Orthodox priests are very careful with throwing their authority around. I thought if I put it back on him in a way that he must use his spiritual authority over me that it might throw him off and get us off the hook.

There was a twinkle in his eye and I knew I was screwed.

Authority was the key issue with me converting to Orthodoxy. Who was in charge of my spiritual life? Me? God? How does that work?

As a Protestant, I had thrived on that spiritual rugged-individualism. A personal and literal interpretation of the Bible and a defiant nature that no one was able to tell me what ministry to do or how to apply the Bible or what to believe was my core attribute, my American virtue. I was an American after all. I was a seminarian too. I had pulled myself up by my own spiritual bootstraps. I was a spiritual militant libertarian revolutionist. The 'don't tread on me' mentality seemed to be a root cause of my spiritual head injuries. I knew from seminary that if I was in charge of how to interpret the Bible and hence my spiritual life then I was in charge of everything. I didn't have to submit to anybody if I didn't agree with them. Except when it came to the date of Easter—I listened to the pope on that one.

However, the different and healing Orthodox spirituality required humble obedience first. In this new spirituality I was no longer in charge. I had to trust and obey a real live spiritual authority. An authority that had inferior knowledge of the Bible than me but superior wisdom in the ways of God.

"I am *telling* you to do this, with my full support and God's grace, you will do just fine," our priest said.

I humbly submitted, thanked our priest and went home wishing I hadn't thrown all my Protestant Christian Education books from the seminary in the dumpster.

∞

As superintendents we inherited a Church school program that was forty years behind the evolution of 'Sunday school'ology' in Protestantism. Orthodox Church school programs looked like a nineteen fifties public elementary school with chalk boards, booklets requiring rote memorization of everything, quizzes and even a snack time. This was fine for the nineteen fifties American Protestant congregations but I had been involved in the future of youth ministry at the mega-church with multi-media jumbotron worship experiences and espresso stations. I was on the cutting edge of youth ministry for the post-modern 'emergent church' Christian youth.

I was put in a tough spot so with God's help and the priest's full support I did what any former Protestant youth group leader with spiritual head injuries would do—I implemented a reformation. I instituted major reforms to the program and rewrote the rules of how Church school was to be done.

I renamed it Sunday school. I held mandatory Sunday school teacher meetings about how to 'experientially' teach and make the faith 'real-life' for the kids. If you missed three meetings you would be asked to resign your teaching position. (Heretics will be burned at the stake!) I no longer required children to sit with their classes during Liturgy but would now have them sit with their families. (Individuals trump institutions) I did away with all attendance awards and special academic recognitions that would create competitiveness among the children. (Authentic participation trumps awards and prizes) I required lesson plans for the whole year so I could later rewrite the curriculum. I had one-on-one performance reviews with the teachers. I established a weekly Sunday school wide assembly where I could cast my vision, inspire and preach a little lesson to the children. It was an awesome reformation. I ripped the bandages off my wounds and I channeled Martin Luther; no John Calvin; no wait, I channeled one of the more radical and dangerous reformers of all time, my old self.

∞

St. Nicholas day (Dec 6) is a special day for our parish because he is our patron Saint and there are special celebrations and festivities on that Sunday. So I decided to change my sermon model assembly and début my acting skills. I acted out a scene from St. Nicholas's life.

There is a famous story when St. Nicholas threw bags of gold through a man's window to save him from selling his daughters into prostitution. I had a reversed Crown Royal purple velvet bag filled with golden foiled chocolate coins as a prop. I acted out the scene three times and threw the liquor bag into the group of kids sitting on the floor. The younger children laughed and thought it was filled with real coins and the older children stared blankly at me, unresponsive; probably thinking, who is this fool?

At the end of the skit, I was going to give the chocolate coins to the children for them to remember the love and charity exampled by St. Nicholas. What I did not count on was the questions from the sweet innocent children at the end of my brief one man show.

'Why did the dad have to sell his daughters?'—'How do you sell a daughter, Mr. Olson, like, what's to sell?' The questions snowballed on me.

I knew at that moment God's grace had been made perfect in my weakness because I had botched the whole thing up.[80] How do you explain a sex slave trade and survival prostitution to a bunch of pre-pubescent holy little children? You don't. You abruptly end the Q & A by giving out candy and hope your teachers don't kill you after class.

---

[80] "And He said to me, 'My grace is sufficient for you, for My strength is made perfect in weakness.' Therefore most gladly I will rather boast in my infirmities, that the power of Christ may rest upon me" (2 Corinthians 12:9).

My 'Orthodox-Protestant hybrid reformation' was a glorious failure. My spiritual head injuries were in full blown infection and caused me to dread coming to church. I was well intended and acting out of obedience but virtue was not being displayed.

∞

I know—don't be so hard on yourself; some of that stuff was good—the problem with my reformation was Orthodoxy has a whole different orientation towards life, spirituality and experiencing God. I couldn't retro fit a Protestant pedagogy into Orthodoxy. I should have served my teachers and encouraged every single child with words of love and humor and not changed a thing. Instead I was not only misdiagnosing the problem with Orthodox Church school but was guilty of spiritual malpractice. Luckily, my reformation didn't catch on and I was not asked or told to be the superintendent again and God worked everything out anyway.

For years I was worried that I had done great harm to my Church family. As part of my self-given penance for trying to start a reformation of the Church school program, I decided to read through the entire curriculum resources and archdiocese education department's 'recommended reading'. I stumbled on a truly remarkable book.

The book was <u>Foundations for Orthodox Christian Education</u> by John Boorjamra. It is a book about how Orthodox in America should teach their youth the Orthodox faith. Boorjamra was before his time generationally. It is the single most revolutionary piece of writing for Orthodox youth education available today, in my humble and flawed spiritually head injured opinion. I am no longer in the Church school game but if I was spiritually directed and had to be the superintendent again I would be a Boojamraite reformer.

I would focus on getting the kids to 'know' the faith by learning from people who have lived it. No convert under ten years in Orthodoxy would be a teacher and no one under the age of thirty. The curriculum would flow with the liturgical calendar and would include not only going to matins and vespers but understanding the structure of the services. The icons and the lives of the saints would be the classroom books and discussion topics. Lessons would be centered on how ones Orthodox spiritual practices prepare the children to handle life as they will experience it and how to pray, serve and love one another. Programs will always fail where communal prayer and acts of love will always succeed.

'The Way, the Truth and the Life',[81] is an encounter and inclusion in the spiritual/physical manifestation of the Body of Christ—the one holy catholic and apostolic historically instituted Church. There is no program or a certain amount of knowledge memorized or an individual set of beliefs held together in common with others spirituality that can bring about this 'way', this 'truth', this 'life'. There is no way to performance manage or conjure up spirituality. It requires the means of grace offered by God via prayer, sacraments, acts of love and communal corporate worship.

---

[81] "Jesus said to him, "I am the way, the truth, and the life'" (John 14:6).

Orthodox spirituality is like a life-long dance with the Trinity on the dance floor of Holy Tradition. The Church school's reason for existence is to teach the children the music and the steps to this divine dance and then get them on that dance floor not to create a supplemental program to the divine services. The future of Orthodoxy hangs on the young learning how to live Orthodox lives from its elders, who have been spiritually dancing for decades. The older generations have grown virtues and danced with God much longer than some newbie radical reformer who acts like a saint holding a Crown Royal bag and gives out candy to get out of some accidental sex trade lesson. We need people who have the virtues of St. Nicholas, the patron saint of children, to teach us all how to live and love and dance.

r. leo olson

ST. EPHREM'S LINE DANCING

During Great Lent[82] there is a wonderful prayer credited to St. Ephrem.[83] We say it together during the Wednesday night service, call Pre-Sanctified Liturgy:[84]

> O Lord and Master of my life, take from me the spirit of sloth, faintheartedness, lust of power, and idle talk. **(Prostration)**

> But give rather the spirit of chastity, humility, patience and love to your servant. **(Prostration)**

> Yes, O Lord and King, grant me to see my own sin and not to judge my brother, for You are blessed from all ages to all ages. Amen. **(Prostration)**

---

[82] A forty day period (before Easter) when Orthodox Christians fast from meat and animal products, pray more and give alms or money to the poor.

[84] Ephrem (306-376) wrote a wide variety of hymns, poems, and sermons in verse, as well as prose biblical exegesis for practical edification of the church in troubled times. Ephrem's works witness to an early form of Christianity. He has been called the most significant of all of the fathers of the Syriac-speaking Church tradition.

This prayer contains a wonderful summation of Orthodox spirituality and it has become the prayer of my life. There is no other prayer I need to pray for healing from my type of spiritual head injuries.

One reason I like it is because it has Protestant power words all over it: 'Master of my life' and 'Lust for power' and 'sloth' and the most guilt tripping phrase for me, 'not to judge my brother', plus you get to literally fall on your face before the altar of God. The last phrase of the prayer always sends me to a prostration of the heart for it is the core of my spiritual head injuries—it has become an 'altar call' I gladly prostrate forward for with head bowed and eyes closed.

As a former Protestant, I was trained to argue the finest points of a doctrinal statement; convince people to conform to a Christian code of conduct with biblical proof-texts and make snap judgments of others:

> —*Saved* because they asked Jesus into their heart and faithfully attended both services on Sunday or *lost* because they don't go to a Bible believing church or were entangled in the sinful culture.
>
> —Socially *liberal* because they went to the movies or *conservative* because they waited for the home video.
>
> —From a *back-slidden' family* because their dad went to a bar on a Friday night or a *right with the Lord family* because he attended the Saturday morning men's breakfast.

—'On fire for the Lord' because they sat in the front row during service or *lukewarm*—in danger of being vomited out of the Lord's mouth[85]—because they often snuck into the back row of the service late.

I was told it was not judging others but 'fruit inspecting'. Taken from the letter to the church in Galatia where St. Paul compares vices and virtues called fruit.[86] So it was not considered judging others to inspect the *fruit* of their life by their social activities. The problem for me was as soon as I did that I could not help but compare myself to those 'bad apples' and then assure myself that I was not as rotten as those other poor souls.

When you're raised with this type of 'spiritual fruit inspecting' and then confronted every Great Lent with this powerful and humbling prayer, it's as if I am living out the

---

[85] "I know your works, that you are neither cold nor hot. I could wish you were cold or hot. So then, because you are lukewarm, and neither cold nor hot, I will vomit you out of My mouth" (Revelation 3:15-16 - Jesus to the Church at Laodicea).

[86] "Now the works of the flesh are evident, which are: adultery, fornication, uncleanness, lewdness, idolatry, sorcery, hatred, contentions, jealousies, outbursts of wrath, selfish ambitions, dissensions, heresies, envy, murders, drunkenness, revelries, and the like; of which I tell you beforehand, just as I also told you in time past, that those who practice such things will not inherit the kingdom of God. But the **fruit** of the Spirit is love, joy, peace, longsuffering, kindness, goodness, faithfulness, gentleness, self-control" (Galatians 5:19-13).

parable of the Publican and the Pharisee.[87] The Pharisee looked over at the Publican or sinner and inspected the fruit of his life and prayed 'down' on him, 'At least I'm not like that poor bastard'. (Paraphrasing here) The poor bastard fell to his knees and begged God saying, 'God be merciful to me a sinner'. For my particular spiritual head injuries, kneeling, face to the ground, only looking at my own fruit or lack thereof actually helps the healing process and why I love St. Ephrem's prayer so much.

∞

My first few times through Great Lent, this prayer along with its three prostrations became almost comical and confusing due to the general lack of athleticism of Orthodox Christians. The brunt of the blame rests in the fact that most American Orthodox Church buildings have pews in the nave. Now don't misunderstand me, I like my pew to be warm and cushioned. It helps comfort me especially when I have the *spirit of sloth, and faintheartedness*. However, this pew jostling does give opportunities to witness the 'St. Ephrem's line dance' in all its two left-footed awkwardness and liturgical immodesty.

The lights were dim but not too dim to not glow off the gold leafed icons in the dome of St. Nicholas during this one particular evening service. The red fire of St. Elijah's chariot

---

[87] "The Pharisee stood and prayed thus with himself, 'God, I thank You that I am not like other men—extortioners, unjust, adulterers, or even as this tax collector" (Luke 18: 11; full parable is vs.9-14).

icon appeared as real fire, St. Nicholas on the iconostasis[88] stoically looked on, the Pangaea,[89] the biggest icon of Mary with baby Jesus on her lap—front and center in every Orthodox Church, offered her spacious embrace to everyone present. The incense added to the 'cloud of witnesses'[90] that have lovingly watched us, interceded for and continually root for us to not lose heart during the bittersweet marathon of Great Lent: St. John Maximovitch whose incorrupt body I've actually seen in San Francisco one summer; St. Mary of Egypt, the desert harlot that was transformed into a most holy woman who walked on water, was befriended by a lion and fought demons who tortured her with lust-filled memories for seventeen years; the brilliant and bold St. Mark of Ephesus who defended 'no fire' in purgatory and illumined the Orthodox understanding of the intermediate state of the soul after death; St. John the Damascene who summarized Orthodox Christianity so the blind Saul's of the world could

---

[88] The large wall of icons that separates the sanctuary, proper, from the nave, where the people assemble.

[89] Panagia or Platytera (Greek: Πλατυτέρα; "wider" or "more spacious") is an icon of the Theotokos, facing the person directly, usually depicted full length with her hands open, and with the image of Christ as a child in front of her chest, also facing the person directly. It's usually the biggest icon in the Church building. It also is the most inviting and evangelical- Mary had Christ IN her physically and spiritually as all Christians are called to have Christ in them. Poetically, by containing the Creator of the Universe in her womb, Mary has become *Platytera ton ouranon*, which means: "More spacious than the heavens."

[90] "Therefore we also, since we are surrounded by so great a **cloud of witnesses**, let us lay aside every weight, and the sin which so easily ensnares us, and let us run with endurance the race that is set before us" (Hebrews 12:1).

see Christ like St. Paul did; St. Mary Magdalene who was healed by Christ of her seven personal demons, remained at the foot of the cross when others fled, and was the very first person to see the resurrected Christ; St. Raphael of Brooklyn who traveled the railways of early America and established twenty nine parishes—'sacramental stations' for the brave immigrants who established an Orthodox presence in the new world; Sts. Gregory of Nyssa, Basil and Gregory of Nazianzus, the Cappadocian fathers, whose communal friendship shaped Orthodox Trinitarian theology and monasticism; St. Benedict, our Latin (Catholic) saint who has taught us that it takes constant prayer and hard work to live a truly Christocentric life, and many many others all there with us in spirit and icon every day—truly a great cloud of witnesses.

The chanter was spot-on, the minor tones reverberated in my heart and I hummed along—off key. The eyes of the angels in the dome came alive as heaven and earth co-mingled again. Sacred time and space—the Kingdom of God, had manifested again claiming prominence in my attention from the profane culture I had encountered earlier that day in the cut throat world of real estate sales.

The first of three St. Ephrem's prayers came upon us in the service and it caught some off guard. The Protestant 'converts' had anticipated the prayer and moved to the aisle for room to fall to the ground in humility. I am one of them—I need some elbow room to really get down and humble.

The prayer was rolling off the tongue of the priest at a good speed...*O Lord and Master of my life, take from me the spirit of sloth, faintheartedness, lust of power...*I jockeyed for position in the center aisle. It was packed. The priest was saying the prayer so fast that I misjudged my distance from the woman in front of me. As we both dropped to our knees she adjusted back half a step and my head hit her rump. It was slight but we both knew it. She apologized under her breath. I was horrified and embarrassed.

The second prostration was quickly upon us and I squirmed for more room. I turned to look over my shoulder. A woman with a short skirt was somehow managing the prostration but desperately pulling at her skirt fighting for modesty. Can't go over there, she's going to lose that modesty battle, I think, so I just stood there. For the final prostration I slid back in the pew and did 'the hand to the forehand to the ground-leaning sideways' in the pew prostration. This move is like liturgical break-dancing and the whole place looks like some disorganized flash-mob.

After the first prayer was over and the faithful were re-seated, I exited the pew and faked a bathroom trip. I stood in the vestibule in front of the ornate icon of St. Nicholas. I started to talk to him or myself—it was one of those weird times in your head when you aren't sure it's prayer or your own mind reasoning. I'm actually sad that I can't even focus on THE prayer of Great Lent because of a head-butt and someone's immodest skirt. I am about to 'inspect some fruit' when I remembered the last part of the prayer. *Don't judge just kneel*—and the first blow of my need for repentance during Great Lent had struck me hard. These spiritual blows happen every Great Lent and they are devastating to my often slothful spiritual attitude and self-love. However, they are essential for my healing, like cauterizing a wound.

I re-entered the nave and sat in the back corner where there was more room to prostrate. After several minutes of re-booting my mind and heart into the service, a late comer arrived and made me slide into the center of the pew. I smiled and slightly bowed my head but wondered if she was going to be a 'pew blocker' and not let me out to prostrate.

The second time we prayed St. Ephrem's prayer was upon us and the pew blocker didn't make a move for the aisle. There I stood too frustrated to do the sideways pew-prostration, so I watched the chaos. People stumbled over each other to get to the aisle to prostrate. Some were early, some were late, some reconsidered and sat down. It's a bad line dance—like a group 'Electric Slide' to the wrong song.

I excused myself from taking communion that night. I was soured inside. So I decided to stand the rest of the service as penance. I watched as my brothers and sisters in Christ communed. I reassured myself that I was connected to them by the Eucharist and must rely on their prayers and humble prostrations for strength to make it until the next time the healing spiritual Medicine of the soul was offered.

My spiritual head injuries often lead me to have some strange mental battles. There was an authentic, mystical, purgatorial type of battle raging inside of me. My own personal inner universe was under attack. This has happened to me regularly, especially during Great Lent. It's hard to put into words. I think of it as a dance with the Divine, but I seem to always be off beat or I step on the Holy Spirit's toes. I trip over grace in the day to day footwork and I thank God the dance of Great Lent is only forty days long because my dancing looks more like wrestling with God and I usually get my spiritual ass kicked, like Jacob the dreamer.[91]

∞

After I head-butted that woman I felt insecure about physical acts of worship. I also couldn't stop watching the visual oddities and chaos during our services.

The first thing I noticed was the speed in which people genuflected or crossed themselves. The motion of the 'speed cross' was almost circular and obviously focused on being able to cross oneself three times in the time it took another person to cross oneself once. I also noticed that some people did a deep bow, touching the ground and crossed their whole body. This is called a *metania* and is a prostration bowing-combo move. It has freaked out many Protestants who have misinterpreted the move as 'bowing to idols'.

When people crossed themselves was fairly uniform— when the priest tossed the censer smoke at you, and when 'Father, Son, and Holy Spirit' was said. The confusing thing was that people randomly added 'crossings' when the Liturgy hit on a special moment for them. Some people crossed themselves over fifty times during a service. I wondered if I was missing some special moment or was this just personal piety.

---

[91] Tells a fascinating story of how Jacob wrestled with an angel or a preincarnate manifestation of God all night and had his hip dislocated. (Ref. Genesis 32:22-32)

The third thing I noticed was that no one really knew when to stand, sit or kneel during any given service. It's comical as we all looked at each other for permission to sit. When people looked at me I just smiled and shrugged my shoulders. When no one leads it's really bad line-dancing.

I observed many other liturgical movements and tried to determine the right and wrong way to physically worship. The soreness from my spiritual head injuries started to throb as confusion and pride of not looking stupid occupied my mind rather than simply worshipping God. Later, that Great Lent I decided to accept and celebrate the diversity of movements and not judge my brother's liturgical dance moves. The lesson was once again, not about me. In the end I saw the beauty in the chaos.

∞

The physicality of worship in the Orthodox Church is a visual expression of how the Incarnation[92] changed everything and a way for me to get my faith out of my head. The implications of the incarnation are absolutely necessary for the healing of my spiritual head injuries. I can no longer just sing a praise song about humility with eyes closed and hands raised

---

[92] The theological teaching that Jesus as the second person in the triune God became human, incarnated. By uniting the Divine with the created order He transformed and redeemed all aspects of the physical creation. Everything in the profane physical world has the potential to be made sacred, infused with Divine Energy—eating, drinking wine, washing, sleeping, fishing, speaking, working and even social gatherings, like the wedding at Cana. (John 2:1-12)

and have an emotional feel good moment. I now must literally and physically bow my head and take my fruit inspecting eyes off others and fall face down to the ground in humble adoration.

If I really believe that Jesus Christ, the second person of the eternal Trinity, One God, came to earth and dwelt among us then I should rightly fall to my face, cross myself as fast as I can and kneel before Him at every opportunity. That's what Orthodox worship is all about anyway—encountering the risen Lord in a real spiritual and physical sense. We sin physically, so we should worship physically. We all fight a thousand battles in our personal lives and each are injured by sin. Just because I may liturgically dance oddly doesn't mean that I should get in the way of others or concern myself with 'inspecting the fruit' of their worship.

I really did see the beauty in the chaos that Great Lent, and I reminded myself that spiritual/physical instincts will take over when Christ is present. If He really is present, if I'm really in tune with that reality and not head-butting or skirt glancing, I will act appropriately and my worship will be well received by the Reader of Hearts.

So whether I bow, make a metania, kneel with a one-knee football stance, lean down in a sideways hand to floor in the pew maneuver, or a full body/floor prostration—I hope what He really sees is a broken and contrite heart that is humbly face down when He is present.[93] And He is always present.

---

[93] "The sacrifices of God *are* a broken spirit, a broken and a contrite heart—these, O God, You will not despise" (Psalm 51:17).

r. leo olson

FATHER TIME
DOESN'T WEAR A WATCH

The perceptibly mundane gathering Tuesday through Friday at St. Nicholas Orthodox Church in Grand Rapids for the daily matins service is amazingly underestimated for its spiritual benefits. The whole world is prayed for by a few holy old men. Sure the Catholics have Mass every morning all over the city but as far as I know, daily matins at St. Nicholas is the only such gathering of Eastern Orthodox Christians for daily prayer in Western Michigan.

One would think it would be packed, busting at the seams but it's not. In fact I have a hard time waking my own sorry ass soul from the heavy sleep of indolence for attendance. I've had good runs of attendance, usually when I feel particularly repentant, when I am going through a hard time in life, or writing about demons in my novels. I should be at matins more often, if I could only find the time and if I really believed what was going on in the cosmic and spiritual dimensions of God's creation when we pray together. But I'm in recovery from spiritual head injuries. I have seasons of doubt like St. Thomas.[94] At times I am as confused as Simon

---

[94] "Now Thomas, called the Twin, one of the twelve, was not with them when Jesus came. The other disciples therefore said to him, 'We have seen

Magus the Sorcerer[95] about my own spiritual motivations. Consequently, I don't always perceive the worship of the Orthodox Church as the Kingdom of God manifesting itself in temporal time.

Time is a funny thing to think about and soon becomes a mind boggling paradox for me as I unlearn God through Orthodoxy. There are two aspects of time in Orthodox theology, the *chronos* or chronological aspect of time and the *kairos* aspect of time or a moment when something sacred happens in temporal time. Orthodox spirituality has both aspects at work all the time. They work together dynamically to actually redeem the moments that make up our lives by pushing back the profane, and make room to live in the sacred Kingdom of God here on earth. Monks live in these sacred moments regularly and in so doing live like angels. Mind boggling.

Before the Liturgy the deacon says, 'It is time for the Lord

---

the Lord.' So he said to them, 'Unless I see in His hands the print of the nails, and put my finger into the print of the nails, and put my hand into His side, I will not believe'" (John 20: 24-25).

[95] "...And when Simon saw that through the laying on of the apostles' hands the Holy Spirit was given, he offered them money, saying, 'Give me this power also, that anyone on whom I lay hands may receive the Holy Spirit.' But Peter said to him, 'Your money perish with you, because you thought that the gift of God could be purchased with money! You have neither part nor portion in this matter, for your heart is not right in the sight of God. Repent therefore of this your wickedness, and pray God if perhaps the thought of your heart may be forgiven you. For I see that you are poisoned by bitterness and bound by iniquity.' Then Simon answered and said, 'Pray to the Lord for me, that none of the things which you have spoken may come upon me'" (Acts 8: 18-24).

to act.' And then the priest starts the space ship of the nave, heaven and earth co-mingle, and we are caught up, raptured, if you will permit the reclamation of the word, into the *kairos* of the Lord.

Orthodox services are sacred moments when God the Holy Spirit is actually present with us. Still, the watch watchers check their wrists or worse yet their phones because the Liturgy is taking too much *chronos*—Oh, St. Basil, your prayers are so long.[96] I'm guilty of time traveling sins like this—family dinner plans, restaurant reservations, or the Detroit Lions game has an early kickoff. It's shameful. The Lord is acting, redeeming us, redeeming time (our *chronos* and *kairos*) and I can't put away all earthly cares for an hour and fifteen minutes. Lord have mercy. Time, that mind boggling mystery that is all too often in conflict in my life, except at weekday matins at St. Nicholas.

∞

The chapel at St. Nicholas is the size of an elementary classroom separated by an old iconostasis from a previous building. It has a classroom feel to me with the florescent lighting but the stained glass windows off-set that feel and the incense is always thick, which helps too. I like the services to be 'full smokers' so you smell like church after you leave for the battle of the day.

---

[96] St. Basil assembled a Liturgy that has longer prayers for the priest than the Liturgy of St. John Chrysostom. It gives rise to noticeable gaps of silence if the priest doesn't pray them aloud and adds an average of ten to fifteen minutes to the service.

There are many weary and heavy laden people that come from time to time, for different reasons and different seasons. On the left of our small nave of five pews, you can count on at least three elderly gentlemen in their eighties and nineties to be present, every day. I call them the three wise men. They come, usually in suits and ties, long time retired, but still representing a generation that valued formality of dress— they're ninety years old and still wearing neck-ties while I wonder how many times I can wear a pair of jeans before it's considered dirty.

I am early because I'm a former Protestant and converts like me are always early. There was a reward for coming early. It was the blessing of being edified by the idle talk of older men.

It's the same edifying conversation almost every time. One of the wise men, Wilson Yared, is known jestfully as 'Father Time'. He's in charge of declaring when the matins service will start. Our priest, also involved in the idle talk of the old men, defends Father Time's role as the time keeper. The conversation is the same conversation throughout the week. It goes something like this:

Wiseman number one says, "Father, it's about 8:30, don't you think it's time to start?"

Our priest usually stands up from sitting in the front pew and says, "Hold on a second. It's not for you to declare such things."

All of the wise men chuckle and the debate about who is the official time keeper, and digital versus traditional watches, and how we start matins late every day ensues. Eventually one of the wise men calls the debate to order and says, "but now it's actually 8:33."—then tries to show our priest his watch. Our priest will dismissively and playfully wave him off and will have no part of this logic.

He'll say, "It has been long established, due to the fickleness of watches and other such devices that one man is appointed the time keeper and that is Father Time. All chaos will erupt if we start going by some other standard of time."

Everyone present smiles warmly and then will look to Father Time for his declaration. He is hard of hearing and does not wear a watch. Nonetheless, all eyes are on him and then our priest will offer a slight nod. Father Time will announce as only he can do, with his strong, deep voice, "Father, time to get to work!"

I wish everyone could witness this phenomenon of *kairos/chronos* at the daily matins. The love and camaraderie of these men is such a grace to witness. They have all lived, albeit unassumed by them, remarkable lives and their humor is saturated with such strong evidence of a faith-filled rule of life. They make every effort, sometimes with drivers, wheelchairs, walking canes and a host of other mobility aids to gather daily, in that *sacred classroom* space to pray to the God of their fathers for the whole world. Their simple prayers help establish the universe—it's a beautiful paradox of weakness made strong.

Their faithful dedication to their routine is a warm blanket for the sickly soul of a young man like me—a father, husband, self-employed writer, dabbler in real estate, coach for my son's football team, infrequent daily matins attendee and many more demanding titles that fight in *chronos* for my attention. My spiritual head injuries too often let the tyranny of *chronos* squelch the sacred *kairos* throughout my days, my weeks, my months, and my years.

I have realized that young people do not have the same relationship with time as the three wise men at daily matins. They are time travelers and know the secret of how to transcend time and enter the *kairos* of the Lord through a routine of daily prayer. They know that only one thing is needful for the time we are given to live our lives and that is why they are able to sit at the Lord's feet every day.[97]

∞

I think about Father Time and the wise men often. I think about them when I hear the countless present tense proclamations in Orthodox services. "Christ is born! Glorify Him." Not Christ *was* born but *is* born. "Today is the day of salvation", "Today He *is* suspended above the waters", "Christ *is* risen! Truly He *is* risen!"

These time traveling phrases are all over the services and the hymns chanted during matins. It's as if the time space continuum collapses and we are mystically transported into the Kingdom of God where Jesus, the Alpha and Omega, the

---

[97] "But Martha was distracted with much serving, and she approached Him and said, 'Lord, do You not care that my sister has left me to serve alone? Therefore tell her to help me.' And Jesus answered and said to her, 'Martha, Martha, you are worried and troubled about many things. But one thing is needed, and Mary has chosen that good part, which will not be taken away from her'" (Luke 10:40-42).

One who is and was and is to come welcomes us into His presence when two or three are gathered in His Name. *Chronos* and *kairos*—mind boggling, really when you think of it.

Ecclesiastics 3:1-8 is a lovely passage of Scripture and a pretty good rock-n-roll song titled; *Turn, Turn, Turn* by the Byrds:

> [1] To everything there is a season,
> A time for every purpose under heaven:
> [2] A time to be born,
> And a time to die;
> A time to plant,
> And a time to pluck what is planted;
> [3] A time to kill,
> And a time to heal;
> A time to break down,
> And a time to build up;
> [4] A time to weep,
> And a time to laugh;
> A time to mourn,
> And a time to dance;
> [5] A time to cast away stones,
> And a time to gather stones;
> A time to embrace,
> And a time to refrain from embracing;
> [6] A time to gain,
> And a time to lose;
> A time to keep,

And a time to throw away;
[7] A time to tear,
And a time to sew;
A time to keep silence,
And a time to speak;
[8] A time to love,
And a time to hate;
A time of war,
And a time of peace.

Stranded in time, with spiritual head injuries, trying to balance the fractured demands of the many time-tables fighting for my attention has been a struggle for me. I sometimes lose my sense of time, whatever that means. But healing has come from confessing my sins of time, like getting riled up with anger and involving myself in mud-slinging political debates or, watching mindless television, or getting obsessed with conquering all the levels of the video game Angry Birds. I seem to never run out of time to eat, sleep or have sex. But I am slow to commit to regular prayer services like matins, even if the world depends on our prayers which the Orthodox Church teaches.

But I do not lose hope; it takes time to heal. I do not despair when I lose the American lifestyle time battles because the Orthodox Church, clergy, monastics and the laity always pray for me. Also, I have the daily example of the wise men and Father Time, who wears no watch, to aspire to. They remind me that our God is slow to wrath, loves humankind, is always transforming, and healing us. I believe what He really wants me to do is be present, fully present, when He is working and He is working all the time.

r. leo olson

BITE THE SPOON —
DON'T BITE THE SPOON

The most important, sobering, awesome, terrible, life giving event in my life happens when I approach the chalice and am spoon fed the Body and Blood of our Lord. I am mysteriously and sacramentally uniting my life with His. He is literally and physically in me and I am spiritually in Him.[98] It is an event that takes place on earth and in the Kingdom of Heaven at approximately 11:15 a.m. every Sunday morning.

Eucharist taking is a great mystery, incomprehensible but the foundational spiritual reality for Orthodox Christians. I personally believe it is the moment in time when I am most healed from my spiritual head injuries and become truly human.[99] I can be no more human than at that moment of uniting myself to God. It is a sacred mystery where all my ontology, (my being'ness—who am I) my metaphysical beliefs, (what is ultimately real in the universe) and my

---

[98] "He who eats My flesh and drinks My blood abides in Me, and I in him" (John 6:56).

[99] Drawing from Orthodox teachings about Genesis chapters 2 and 3: Adam and Eve in their perfect created state were in full communion with God and walked in the cool of the day with Him. They were Eucharistic creatures, the only creatures able to 'give thanks' (Eucharist) to God for they were both together an icon of God, made in His image and likeness.

epistemological beliefs (how I understand reality) and all those other confusing philosophical terms find meaning, value and make life not seem like an insane mental free for all.

But this sacred rite and means of receiving the grace of God in a true and real way is not a product of my philosophical reasoning but a spiritual reality of my relationship with God. Often I weep when I examine myself and say pre-communion prayers. Not because I feel guilty for my sins but because I see how far I have wandered lost in the desert of my self-love and now hunger and thirst for the life giving Bread of Heaven and living water of this Eucharistic oasis. Every Sunday I mystically and spiritually mourn my own death and am offered life, resurrection, and joy in the communion chalice.

I'm not making it up. How could I? I can't even decide what I want for dinner some nights. Somehow and in so many ways eating at the Lord's Table is re-making me. It's apophatic in nature.[100] I may not be able to understand it with my spiritually injured mind or explain it in exacting theological definitions but I do hope when I make my leap of faith into eternity that I was in relational communion with God. I hope my salvation depends on more than my Bible knowledge and my own personal beliefs about Jesus. I hope I am connected to every person, saint and sinner, who believed the promises of

---

[100] In apophatic or negative theology, it is maintained that we can never truly define God in words. In the end, the believer must transcend words to understand the nature of the Divine. When we attempt to capture it in human words, we inevitably fall short. *Cross reference with cataphatic theology for further understanding.*

Jesus that the Eucharist was a spiritual and physical vehicle for a life giving reality and an eternal union with the Divine.[101] However, as I revel in all those deep and heady thoughts I still seek the answer to the all-important question: Do I bite the spoon or not?[102]

I have taken communion in several different parishes: Greek, Russian, Antiochian, Romanian, and at several archdioceses conventions. I have received Eucharist from deacons, priests, bishops, an archbishop and even at a Liturgy where Patriarch Ignatius the IV of Antioch[103] was serving. I still didn't know what to do at that most intimate and awkward of moments.

Once I visited another parish. I prepared my soul to take communion by reading all the pre-communion prayers and was even early to the matins service before the Divine Liturgy. As I as approached the chalice to be spoon fed the life giving mysteries for the remission of my sins, the priest asked me, "When was the last time you went to confession?"

---

[101] "Then Jesus said to them, 'Most assuredly, I say to you, unless you eat the flesh of the Son of Man and drink His blood, you have no life in you. Whoever eats My flesh and drinks My blood has eternal life, and I will raise him up at the last day. For My flesh is food indeed, and My blood is drink indeed. He who eats My flesh and drinks My blood abides in Me, and I in him. As the living Father sent Me, and I live because of the Father, so he who feeds on Me will live because of Me. This is the bread which came down from heaven—not as your fathers ate the manna, and are dead. He who eats this bread will live forever" (John 6:53-58).

[102] Orthodox Churches mix the bread/Body and wine/Blood into a chalice and spoon feed it to communicates, like little children.

[103] In Orthodoxy the patriarch holds the same position as the pope—they call him the Patriarch of Rome.

I was surprised at this impromptu priestly interrogation as he held the spoon of life in a protective manner. Luckily, I had been to confession the night before after the vespers service at my home parish. I passed his verification standards and leaned my head back waiting for him to deposit the Eucharist in my mouth when he sternly directed me to, "Bite the spoon!" I did with teeth clanking verve.

At another parish I took it upon myself to bit the spoon but held my mouth closed a fraction of a second too long and saw the twinge in the priest's eyes as the spoon clinked on the back of my teeth as he tried to retract the spoon. I heard him whisper, "Don't bite the spoon." I felt so sacramentally stupid.

Obviously I was doing something wrong at the most precious of moments in all of my life. So, when the opportunity came to assist the priest and hold the red cloth, like the altar boys do, I almost jumped the pew in front of me and dashed for the corner of the cloth. I stood there smiling and realized this is the closest I will get to being a priest and helping somebody unite themselves to God by sacrament.

My eyes filled with tears as the beauty of my brothers and sisters in Christ, the children of God, were spoon fed the life giving mysteries. Some smiled. Some of the communicants were tear-filled. Some were serious but had a warm look in their eyes. Some approached, arms crossed leaned their head back and the priest flicked the Eucharist in with laser precision. Some approached and bent to one knee, opened wide and the priest hovered the spoon over their mouth and dumped. Some, having lost nimble mobility, turned their heads sideways and cracked their mouths open and the priest surgically inserted the spoon. Some approached straight forward, bent at the knees and bit the spoon. And one small child, after partaking, snuck around to the back of his family and tried to get seconds. The priest smiled and said, "One per customer," and then blessed the child and nodded him away.

Such variety of practices expressing the inner state of their souls: Tears of joy, humble kneelers, the elderly fighting their physical pains with canes and crutches to bend their necks to the Lord and the zealous youngin' trying to get seconds— "Oh taste and see that the Lord is good!" (Psalm 34:8).

Sometimes I stand in the back and wait to be one of the last to commune. I look up at the large icon of Mary, arms open to all, the chosen of God to have Jesus the God-Man live in her, a most profound example of what a Christian really is. Below her stand two altars. On the wall is an icon of the heavenly altar and in front of that the earthly altar, visually reminding me that both heaven and earth, humans and angels, come together in the Divine Liturgy and worship the loving and healing God of the Universe. The holy royal doors, separating us from the Holy of Holies, are open during communion beckoning us back to the Gates of Paradise to walk with the Second Adam in the cool of the evening.

I am always awestruck by the spiritual beauty of Orthodox worship. The parallels with many universal religious arche- types, meaningful rubrics, and historical continuity with Jewish and early Christian worship always fascinates me. I can think of no other thing more beautiful, healing, and truly divine than to witness how my brothers and sisters in Christ unite themselves to the Lover of mankind both physically and spiritually at the chalice Sunday mornings at approximately 11:15 a.m.

Partaking of the divine, holy, most pure, immortal, heavenly, life-creating, and awesome Mysteries of Christ, with all my fellow brothers and sisters in the Lord has been the single most healing and spiritually authentic practice in my entire life. I wagered everything for a spiritual connection to make sense of my life. Even though I have found it, I still don't know if I should bite the spoon or not. But I do know that there is nowhere else I would rather be, nowhere closer to heaven, nowhere that life makes more sense than standing in front of a chalice and spoon.

IS THAT A DEAD PERSON
IN MATINS?

Prayer is always a nice way to start every day and I was feeling particularly happy because of the summer weather, so I decided to wake my son and make him go with me to spend time with the old wise men and pray the matins service with them. He was enthusiastic about this, as you can imagine. We drove to our parish and he sprinted into the 'big church', to find his altar boy robe. I turned and entered the little side chapel.

In the chapel, in front of the icon of Mary, next to the royal doors was an open casket. It was not empty. An elderly woman was asleep in the Lord right in front of me. I immediately stopped and looked to the three faithful wise men with endearing affection. They did not look back at me. I looked to the Khouria[104] at the chanter's stand and she looked back at me with a slight smile, sensing my hesitation. Then from Archangel Gabriel's door of the iconostasis walked out our priest; I still had not moved.

I felt my son stop right behind me and there we stood; six parishioners, one priest and a dead woman. Silence hung in

[104] Arabic title for a priest's wife. In Orthodoxy the priests can marry and have children. The bishops and monastics are celibates.

the air until our priest said, "I don't think she'll mind if we pray. Do you?"

A little spiritually dazed, I answered with a shake of my head and took my seat opposite the casket. My son changed his usual path and chose the Archangel Michael's door to enter the Sanctuary. The matins service began.

Inconspicuously as I could, I stared at the dead woman. I didn't know her. Was she a shut-in? Was she alone in this world? If the funeral was later today why wasn't there anybody else here? My eyes widened at her chest as I thought I saw her breathing. I always think this when I stare at dead people, some psychological trick of the mind—an innate fear of death or something. 'Lord have mercy' rang out from the chanter and I wondered how the Lord's mercy related to her now.

I studied her face. I thought about her life and the historical events she had witnessed when Father mentioned her in a litany for the dead. From her last name I knew she was a Russian woman, white hair, smartly dressed and she held a little bit of life or something in her face. It wasn't the make-up from the mortician. No—it must have been the residue of virtue. She knew of the Russian revolution and World War II. She made it, she survived those evil times but not death, no one escapes that enemy.

My son was careful to navigate his lantern around the casket as the Gospel was about to be read. I saw him glance sideways at her. I smiled at the contrast of such a young boy, innocent and starting his journey through life hoping to gain entry into the kingdom of God and an old woman at the end of her journey, with a life of sacramental sanctification behind her as she had just entered the Kingdom of God. I turned sideways to face the priest as he censed her, the invisible angels and everyone else in the nave. I got a real good look at her as everyone else watched our priest walk past us in order to finish the rite of censing the entire nave. I couldn't help myself; there was a dead woman in matins.

I looked over at the three wise men standing right in front of the casket and wondered what they thought or felt. Their eyes hardly noticed her. They were old. They often joked of their funerals and have told me on more than one occasion they have lived good lives, fought for their country in World War II, succeeded in business and were okay with death. In fact one of them said he was ready to go anytime and he would die in less than two years.

Why was I so uncomfortable around death? These men continue as they do in every matins service, singing off key, a beat behind the chanter, always stand and sit on cue and follow along in the red service pew book which I'm sure they have memorized by now. I know they will just continue to pray until their dying day.

The theological concept of holy relics,[105] the communion of the saints and how they interact with us has taken a little getting used to and something I've had to unlearn about God and His saints. In Orthodoxy, I have confessed a bodily resurrection in the creed every day. I've read about miracles done at the tombs of saints. I've visited a weeping icon in

---

[105] Often a sainted dead person's bones.

Chicago and even though I can't scientifically explain any of them doesn't mean God can't use holy people or even sacred relics as means of His healing grace. I believe many things I don't understand but it's still uncomfortable to be around a dead person or their bones.

I grew up believing there were no 'cross-overs' between the church on earth and the heavenly saints and angels. All paranormal spirits (ghosts) were demons so when you're dead, you're done. The teachings were pretty cut and dry; when you die you immediately go to heaven if you were saved, or you go to hell if you were not. Death was a constant reminder that you better walk with the Lord on earth rather than run with the devil because hell awaits the unprepared— hell with the 'unquenchable fire, the gnashing of teeth and where the worm dieth not'.[106] Death was the tool used to scare the hell out of you, literally. So in matins when I saw a dead person, I got scared concerning my own life. I have not had enough time to repent, unlearn and heal my soul.

She had her chance and probably fared well, but why has God put me in this existential quandary when I was having a happy, sunny day? 'Let the dead bury the dead' the Lord said. I silenced my mind immediately because I know when I start to fire scriptural bullets that my spiritual head injuries have flared up.

I knew there was deeply profound Orthodox theology concerning the incarnation, salvation of the whole person and

---

[106] "It is better for you to enter into life maimed, rather than having two hands, to go to hell, into the fire that shall never be quenched where 'Their worm does not die and the fire is not quenched...'" (Mark 9: 43-44).

bodily resurrections at the root of all that was happening that day, but I couldn't recall any of it for reassurance. Where was she? Where was her soul? Was she like the good thief and in Paradise with Jesus? Was she in some *toll house*[107] or purgatory, soul sleep, or some other intermediate state? Was she a ghost and watching me right now? I remembered the Bible verse that read, 'to be absent from the body is to be present with the Lord'.[108] I believe this on faith alone, because any other alternative is too frightening. I've regressed to my twelve year old self and was scared of death and hell and those undying worms.

I calmed down and tried to focus my racing mind on the Synaxarion reading.[109] It was filled with stories of gruesome martyrs that day. It was not edifying. I remembered several quotes from the Bible and started to string together a theory that made temporary sense, but when it came to actually praying right next to a dead person, all those Bible verses and theological rationalizing stuttered into silence.

I knew I had to be quiet now and pay attention to what the Lord was trying to teach me. Silence can be very healing and the dead woman knows more about life, death and God than I do right now. I'm here on earth, left with her faith tradition becoming mine, healing from my spiritual head injuries. I

---

[107] An Orthodox speculative theology and metaphor used to describe the intermediate time between ones death and the final judgment of mankind.

[108] "We are confident, yes, well pleased rather to be absent from the body and to be present with the Lord" (2 Corinthians 5:8).

[109] A compilation of recorded details about the lives of the saints and used to commemorate them in services.

cannot find comfort in the Bible or the theology of my past. She looked so peaceful; she was anxious for nothing and glowed of the peace that surpasses all understanding.[110] I was the opposite. I didn't understand anything. I was without peace. I was anxious, burning with fear, trying to quiet my doubts. I didn't know who was more alive her or me.

Matins ended and the priest came out and chatted with the three wise men. They discussed her life and who she knew and where she lived and the funeral arrangements. I reverenced the icon of Christ but skipped the Virgin Mary icon because, well, just because. My son exited the sanctuary, quickly acknowledged the woman who lay at rest and crossed himself as he passed her.

Then it hit me, the three wise men, close to death themselves, were comfortable with the dead woman in matins because they were prepared for death. They were as holy as they could be and have such strong faith that they no longer feared death but looked forward to a new life with God. My priest was his usual calm self because he does what he always does for the living and the dead; he prays for them. My son, initially taken aback at the sight of his first dead person this close up, left matins with a slight nod and a smile at her.

He was born and raised in the Orthodox faith and has not known the fear I was raised with—no undying worms in his nightmares. He must have instinctively known that there was

---

[110] "Be anxious for nothing, but in everything by prayer and supplication, with thanksgiving, let your requests be made known to God; [7] and the peace of God, which surpasses all understanding, will guard your hearts and minds through Christ Jesus" (Philippians 4:6-7).

nothing to fear either. He just prays for people, serves others, has faith that God is involved with everything he does, and crosses himself when something new that he doesn't understand comes his way. It's a beautiful Christian way to live life, it's healthy—uninjured.

The theology of the 'communion of the saints' and how it should be lived out was fearfully and wonderfully exampled for me in the matins that day by the prayers and the sane actions of healthy, loving and wise people. I may never fully understand or be able to 'chapter and verse' the mystery of death, but I now know experientially that the mystery of death is not to be feared by the young, the old or even me, a scared of death and hell, former biblical assassin who liked to wager with God about wasting his life on worldly pleasures. I am now someone who has been reconciled with the One Holy Catholic and Apostolic Church and finds little bits of healing medicines for spiritual head injuries in Her pious, sacramental practices.

As I left for home with my son that day I asked him what he thought about that whole thing.

"It wasn't that weird after we got praying," he said.

"Yeah, I guess Father was right when he said that she wouldn't mind."

We both smiled because nothing more needed to be said.

I keep good company now, in life and in death.

r. leo olson

THE SACREDNESS
OF SUGAR COOKIES

I was standing around talking to our priest after Liturgy one summer Sunday, feeling good about having made our way to Orthodoxy and raising three cradle Orthodox children. Our experience in this parish has been healing and formative for all of us. We have a good priest, amazing icons and chanters. My son was at the Antiochian Village, an Orthodox summer youth camp, where he has made life-long friends from everywhere, grown in understanding his relationship with God, does acts of love sincerely and has avoided the warped 'turn or burn' hell-fire guilt trip salvation sermons of my summer camp experiences. My girls sing Orthodox songs to themselves when they go to sleep. We pray, we love others and we worship God in the manner He has prescribed. Life is good and I am at peace with the cosmos.

My girls came running up to me and I had to referee a dispute. In other words, break up a chic fight right in front of the priest. *Parenting skills on trial now.* Our priest let me fumble this whole thing up. The one sister demands justice, swift and severe, and the other is just too cute to ever punish for anything.

"Girls, we just came from the Eucharist and now you are fighting? Be kind, love one another, act like nice little

215

Orthodox girls," I scolded them. *Why did I say 'Orthodox girls'?*
My spiritual head injury of pride throbbed as I tried to look
good in front of our priest.

"Girls, I have a question for both of you," Father inter-
rupted me—to my relief. He then looked at me, winked and
said, "I'm going to show you how to tell if your girls are truly
good little Orthodox girls."

He had my full attention now.

"Girls, what's the best part about coming to the Liturgy on
Sunday mornings?"

I smirked at my girls proudly, because kids of former
Protestant biblical assassins always know the answer to every
biblical and theological question—it's the Eucharist, of
course. *Lay it on him girls.*

They both say in unison with their high pitched sweet
voices, "Coffee hour!"

"Well, there you have it. They are truly Orthodox," Father said and brushed his hands together and made a graceful
conversational exit.

My girls ran away because the sugar buzz was too strong to
control for more than twenty-five seconds. I stood in the
hallway, miffed. To my left was the nave and sanctuary—
peaceful, solemn, sacred space, still smelling like incense. To
my right was the profane gathering hall, with wine stains on
the carpet and scuff marks on the dance floor. The cacophony
of coffee hour, with multiple conversations and kids running
everywhere like wild animals, caused me to cringe inside.

I scratched my head standing at the crossroads of sacraments and sugar cookies. Father had thrown me a real curve

ball here. He often does this and lets it sit with me for a while. It's wise; it's loving and respectful. I have grown to appreciate his gentle pastoring style. *But my kids are truly Orthodox because coffee hour is the best part of Liturgy?* I didn't even know it was part of the Liturgy.

∞

For the next year, I started to become aware of the coffee hour and its role in the life of my Orthodox parish and my family. One time I noted the non-Lenten foods offered and scarfed down by the spiritually weak. *Anathema!*[111] I yelled inside. How could any true Orthodox eat Colby cheese cubes during Lent? *Shameful.* My assassin skills reared their ugly head and I reminded myself that I've been taught to look at my own plate and not my brother's. Fasting has personal exemptions and we are all fighting different battles in Lent. I tell myself I shouldn't worry about cheese cubes and creamer in the coffee but I still catch myself looking, judging and eventually sampling myself.

During that same Lent I stepped out of the Liturgy to blow my nose. I had been fighting a cold and was in desperate need of the Eucharistic medicine, so I forced myself to go to Liturgy that morning. As I passed the gathering hall I noticed several people preparing food and not in the Liturgy. *Anathema!* I yelled inside. Receiving the Eucharist is the most important moment in the entire week and these people are exchanging it for melon balls. *Anathema! Anathema!*

---

[111] Greek for accursed, banished, excommunicated.

For me the journey to Orthodoxy was a great quest, a spiritual adventure. It was a series of wagers against severe odds. It required social, career and even extended family relationship sacrifices. It was the 'pearl of great price'.[112] It was a costly journey but I risked it all. My reward? The healing power and identity forming Eucharist was my reward.

I had unlearned my understanding of God and Christianity, wagered everything with God and learned to taste and see that the Lord was good. I savored this act of worship above all else because this was how I connected to the Life of God. It was how I joined the mystical, meta-historical, and trans-spatial Body of Christ. It is how I know I'm in Him and He is in me. It's a mysterious-sacred-mystical-physical-spiritual-divine connection. Mellon balls, coffee hour, cheese cubes and sugar cookies. Anathema to them all!

∞

The conversation with my priest about coffee hour and Liturgy caused me some spiritual indigestion. My assassin skills were beginning to lose their atrophy and my tongue was sharpening. I know when this happens my spiritual head injuries have become infected and flared up. So it was time to see my spiritual father, my soul doctor again.[113]

---

[112] "Again, the kingdom of heaven is like a merchant seeking beautiful pearls, who, when he had found one pearl of great price, went and sold all that he had and bought it" (Matthew 13:45-47).

[113] Spiritual fathers are not always the priest at the parish attended.

I explained the situation and my thoughts to my spiritual father and he leaned back in his chair and smiled at me for a moment. He said, "You don't get it because you're a man from the West and these are people from the East. Journey is everything to you. It's a 'meta-narrative', hardwired in you. It's how you organize your life and how you live your life. You quest, you sojourn, everything about you journeys, moves forward, has a destination. It's why you like the <u>Lord of the Rings</u>—life is a journey. Do you know what the 'meta-narrative' for those born and raised with an Eastern mentality is?"

I shake my head, no, but this is making tons of sense to me. I really am obsessed with the Lord of the Rings.

"It's not the *journey* motif; it's the *banquet* that forms their orientation to life. Eastern minded people are going to a banquet with their faith. They don't worry about going to heaven or hell as much as you do with your background. That's 'journey talk, right? Salvation is a journey for you, right?"

"Uh-huh," I said.

"They worry about not being invited to the Banquet of the Lord. They want to be included. To be uninvited is shameful for them. The key is to not think of one 'meta-narrative' as better than the other. You must hold them both in your heart so you know best how to love your brother. How best to pray for them and worship with them. *Journey* talk with Westerners and *banquet* talk with Easterners."

My girls screaming, 'Coffee hour!' jumped to my memory. *Banquet—the best part of Liturgy.* They were truly little

Orthodox girls but they didn't journey like I did. The Eastern Orthodox meta-narrative has formed their faith. It's different than mine. It's incarnational, with food, dancing, laughing, crying and relationship building. It's a relational epistemology of knowing God not a systematic theologizing abstract deity. They live their faith and life as a banquet, a party.

I've spent my life thinking about 'how' to live my faith in a tradition that argued about wine or grape juice for communion and defined their congregations by the proper way to 'live-out their theology' and remain separated in the culture. Baptist don't drink or dance. My girls intuitively know they're at a party in the Kingdom of God. They sing and dance and eat sugar cookies every Sunday at the little after-glow coffee hour party, after the Eucharistic Banquet of the Lord. I found my spiritual father's words a healing salve once again and thanked God for him.

I started to understand the banquet meta-narrative and its joyous spiritual by-products. The mystical and sacramental act of partaking of the Body and Blood of Christ is called a mystical supper, a Eucharistic meal or the Lord's Supper— banquet language. The liturgical calendar, which is the rhythm and flow of Orthodox spirituality, is a cycle of fasting and feasting. We fast before communion then feast at the coffee hour. We fast from meat and other animal products for forty days during Great Lent then break out the bacon at Pascha! The Feast of Feasts! The Banquet of Banquets!

My journey was now to the banquet of the Lord. I started to relax, put some ice on my spiritual head injuries, enjoyed a cup of coffee and learned to love my brothers and sisters in

Christ from the East, at the coffee hour, one of the best parts of Sunday mornings.

r. leo olson

MISSING THE MOUTH

It was Christmas morning and Sunday. This year I half-heartedly battled the commercialization of the Christmas season. I had kept pretty close to the rule of the Nativity fast.[114] I had been to a couple of family Christmas parties before the 25th because it's so hard for my Protestant family members to appreciate the rhythm and flow of fasting in the liturgical calendar, which has become the rhythm of my personal relationship with God. Sadly, every year I seem to have less and less in common with my family and Protestant friends when it comes to how to prepare and celebrate Christian holidays or Feast days as Orthodox call them. I have long stopped taking friendly fire shots comparing Orthodoxy and it's historically enriched practices and traditions against the strangeness of the commercialization of 'Elf yourself' Christmas cards stuck on everyone's refrigerators. I now try to participate in their expressions and celebrations of the faith, as best I can. Jesus is the reason for the season after all.

This snowy Christmas morning, before the Christmas Liturgy, my kids were extra excited to rip open their pre-

---

[114] Like Great Lent, Orthodox Christians fast from all meats and animal products, pray more and give alms to the poor 40 days before Christmas. It's often referred to as the *Winter Lent*.

sents. Before my wife and I let them go at it, I reminded them that God gave us the most precious gift of all, wrapped in swaddling clothes. They don't listen to this tired old speech. Their little eyes were distracted by the tinsel, wrapping paper, bows and the piles of batteries they saw bursting from their stockings.

I looked to my wife, smiled and said, "Are you sure you want to go to Liturgy?"

She understands the silent struggle I have every dark December of fighting the 'What do you want for Christmas?' consumerism during the Nativity fast and then on the 26th Christmas is over! I've battled to keep Christmas at bay during the fast and now it's as if I showed up to the party as it was ending and have no society at large to celebrate the twelve days of the Christmas feast with.[115] The radio stops playing the Christmas carols, the Christmas trees are all out on the curb in their white recycle friendly bags. Christmas is done too soon.

The kids were excited about their gifts but murmurs of going to Liturgy gained consensus in the three little spoiled rotten cherubs. They're good kids, really, born into an ancient faith tradition with dusty blond hair, greenish-blue eyes and Scandinavian last names. My wife and I believed deeply that joining Orthodoxy was the greatest gift we have given our kids and so there is no negotiating Feast day Liturgies and they know this. The murmurs about not going

---

[115] The 12 days of Christmas are the 12 days between the Feast of Nativity (Christmas) and Theophany or Epiphany (Baptism of Christ)—Dec 26-Jan 6.

quickly changed to trying to bring some of their gifts with them; 'only for the car ride' became their compromising slogan. We allowed it since we had managed to somewhat prepare ourselves for the Eucharist with fasting and prayers that morning.

Off we went.

There was no choir that morning of which I was a little dismayed, but our parish is blessed with several chanters who humbly and beautifully chant. A smattering of lay people polka dot the nave and try to offer chanting support but really it's a bad echo because no one knows the words or Byzantine tones to Orthodox Christmas hymns. We do know several Paschal hymns but Nativity hymns, well, let's just say without congregational singing most of us will just hum along with the chanters and sing the American Protestant carols afterward.

We sat in the front row off to the right side. My Christmas wish was that the deep musical bond of these ancient praises and the teachings of the Incarnation redeeming the universe will give my children a spiritual intuition to use as a guide when they have to navigate the political correctness of 'holiday trees' and endure the ridiculous mocking caricature of St. Nicholas (Santa) in the future. The feast of the Nativity is so much more than Christmas.

St. Basil's Liturgy with the priest reading the extra-long prayers out loud is always stirring for me. I looked down at my youngest daughter who was not engaged mentally with the Liturgy. She stared off into space, I'm sure thinking about her toys just waiting for her at home. I leaned down and asked her if I could hold her for communion today. Her mother is her favorite and often this request is flatly and firmly denied. But not this day—a special little Christmas gift for me. I have maybe one year left of holding my daughter due to her growing up and I smiled at the granted request, as did my wife.

Everyone finished reciting in unity, St. John Chrysostom's pre-communion prayer—the one where we all claim to be the 'chief of sinners' and then almost elbow each other and jockey to be first in line to consume the Lord in the Christmas communion chalice. Thank God we have ushers to make sure a protocol is followed and to keep the cutters at bay and the mystical tension tempered.

I scooped up my daughter, Sophia Nicole, and walked into the aisle.

There were two chalices that morning and we got in the line to the right. Emily, my wife was in front of me, hands on my other daughter Cecelia's shoulders. I was holding Sophia so tight our cheeks touched and she hugged me back; another rare event for someone with sensory integration issues and generally avoids being touched by anyone at all costs. I am in love all over again with my daughter.

I heard the priest say, "The handmaiden of God Emily receives the Body and Blood of Christ for forgiveness of sins and life eternal."

She bent down, tilted her head back and awkwardly waited for the spoon. I wondered if I looked that awkward when I take communion. Then something unfortunate happened.

The priest missed her mouth.

Missing the mouth happens from time to time, a spill

down the side of the cheek, a little left on a beard perhaps or even some of the Holy Eucharist on the red cloth that the altar boys hold up to every chin. But this time all fail-safes had failed. This was a big deal and Sophia and I had a front row view to what happened next.

The priest asked Emily in a sober tone, "Where is it?"

She looked down and pointed to the tile floor.

He then gave two commands, one to her, "Step aside."

The second to the altar boy, "Hold this."

He handed him the chalice and spoon.

The priest then fell to his knees, vestments crumpled, and he lowered his face to the ground and licked up the Body and Blood. He did this thoroughly then resumed his post distributing the Eucharist to Sophia and me.

I walked away reeling internally with what had just happened. Sophia whispered in my ear, "That was sick. He licked the floor." At which I immediately responded, "No Sophia that was beautiful."

I stood there for the rest of the service thinking about what had transpired. The service concluded and we were wished a Merry Christmas and a couple of Orthodox Christmas cheers of, "Christ is born! Glorify Him!" Then we were dismissed.

I stayed behind pretending to make sure my family didn't leave any of the presents that were not supposed to be brought into Liturgy and pondered what I experienced just moments before. I looked up at the large Nativity icon on the wall; it was silent in the nave and it smelled like Church.

Christ came down from heaven and humbled himself to become a nomadic baby, on the run, in harm's way from

Herod. He condescended, became one of us, incarnate from the Virgin Mary and the Holy Spirit so we could unite ourselves to Him, in our humble sinful state.

There is no *cross* without a *cradle*. Angels have longed to look into the mysteries of the incarnation and salvation,[116] and yet here I stood, united to Jesus Christ who made the universe, was born of a virgin and lives in me because of our Eucharistic sacramental fellowship. I looked at the floor where the priest, dressed in gold, an icon of Christ to the parish, humbled himself and licked the floor before my feet.

I was undone inside and tears welled in my eyes. I was reminded of what I was missing when I wagered with God for my life so many years ago on that dock. When I left behind the promises of a career in Protestant Christendom and joined the historical and apostolic Orthodox Church; I was missing the virtue of humility. First lovingly shown to the world by Christ coming to live among us and today, imitated beautifully by one of His priests at the Christmas Divine Liturgy.

I had come a long way in unlearning the scary version of God others had created for me from the Bible. My guns were rusty and my skills as a biblical assassin had atrophied while I have limped along for years now in Orthodoxy, hindered by

---

[116] "Of this salvation the prophets have inquired and searched carefully, who prophesied of the grace *that would come* to you, searching what, or what manner of time, the Spirit of Christ who was in them was indicating when He testified beforehand the sufferings of Christ and the glories that would follow. To them it was revealed that, not to themselves, but to us they were ministering the things which now have been reported to you through those who have preached the gospel to you by the Holy Spirit sent from heaven—things which angels desire to look into" (1 Peter 1:10-13).

the scars of my spiritual head injuries. No theology or Bible verse or philosophical treatise could prepare me for the divine epiphany of that Christmas morning. I was changed, saved, healed after the priest licked the floor, a living synergy of divine humility infused in a humanly flawed priest. As he served me the life giving Eucharist I knew it was God daring me to go and do likewise. Go and leave behind the scars, the bitterness, the regret, the pride, make no more wagers, and let love for others and authentic humility be your first instinct.

I had witnessed the heart of God that day—an epiphany.

An Orthodox Nativity Hymn

Today is born of the Virgin, Him Who holdest all

creation in the hollow of His hand.

He Whose essence is untouchable is wrapped

in swaddling clothes as a babe.

The God Who from of old established the heavens

lieth in a manger.

He Who showered the people with manna in the

wilderness feedeth on milk from the breasts.

And the bridegroom of the Church calleth the Magi,

and the Son of the Virgin accepteth gifts from them.

We worship Thy Nativity, O Christ.

Show us also Thy divine Epiphany!

r. leo olson

A KIERKEGAARDIAN SANDWICH

In seventh grade I had a fifth period class that required me to go across Johnson street in Caledonia to the high school. After class I went to the bathroom then headed back across the street to the junior high building. As I walked through the sleepy little part of town I noticed there was no one around. My white Swatch watch kept good time so I wasn't late but there was no one around, not a soul.

Dread filled my young heart. It started to race. I stood at the cross walk and waited for a car to pass. None did. I saw birds. I saw grasshoppers. I turned around and looked back at the high school. Ghost town.

I crossed the street at a quick pace looked at the two junior high buildings. All was quiet. I was terrified. I ran to the building. I thought the rapture had happened and I was left behind. I started to cry and pray but mostly cry.

I flung open the door and ran to the nearest classroom.

Class had started. My peers were sitting at their desks. The hallways were empty but there were people here. I looked at the clock on the wall—those school clocks that clicked when the minute hand advanced. It clicked. I looked at my Swatch watch and realized my battery had died. I was not left behind to face the tribulation alone just late for class.

"Deep within every human being there still lives the anxiety over the possibility of being alone in the world, forgotten by God, overlooked among the millions and millions in this enormous household. One keeps this anxiety at a distance by looking at the many round about who are related to him as kin and friends, but the anxiety is still there, nevertheless, and one hardly dares think of how he would feel if all this were taken away."[117]

The unspoken 'anxiety' that Kierkegaard speaks of has been mitigated in my life by the realization that I am not alone in this world with all its evil, suffering, horrible uncertainty and constant fear of being alone or even being left behind. Some people really like to be alone but very few like to be left alone, forgotten, not wanted around, that's a different kind of aloneness especially if we think God is the one leaving us alone. We all desire to be loved by God, to be made new by God and recreated for eternal life with God by His divine energies, even if we are unfamiliar with that language.

For me, I had to first unlearn God as a concept, a sum of theological statements, a subjective conglomeration of Bible verses all held together by a fear of hell, performance anxiety, and eternal insecurities all wrapped up in a nice fundamentalist Protestant culture. I had to repent from the

---

[117] Soren Kierkegaard, *The Concept of Dread* (from the Journals, VIII 1 A 363)

god I had learned and co-created. A version of God that isolated me from others by theological exactness and a moral superiority complex.

I could not have re-learned God without being accepted into a community of love. God is a community of love, a Trinity of love. I John 4:7 reads, "God is love"—so simple yet so radically transforming if someone learns this first.

To love God I needed to be loved by others. I needed to experience being the 'Beloved' so I could be like the Lover of mankind and truly love others. Then, and only then, could I feel God through inexplicable, spiritual, sacramental and mystical experiences of the divine energies. Then, and only then, could I connect with God by loving others.

I believe Eastern Orthodoxy is a divine invitation to anyone looking for that kind of communal love, spiritual healing and divine connection. Jesus summed up everything when He said, "Love God and love your neighbor."[118] And it is precisely this manifestation of God as love and His living and loving saints that seduced me into the Eastern Orthodox Church.

I don't hate the Bible or Baptists nor make any triumphant claims about Orthodoxy over other mysterious ways in which God reconciles us—every human to Himself. I just could not stand alone on the B-I-B-L-E. I was soul sick. I needed the help, the teachings, and the traditions from the saints who had lived this Christian life before me. I needed to experience and encounter truth beyond my mental constructs and spiritual

---

[118] "So he answered and said, 'You shall love the LORD your God with all your heart, with all your soul, with all your strength, and with all your mind, 'and 'your neighbor as yourself'" (Luke 10:27).

imaginings. I needed to be saved from the ocean of spiritual uncertainty and board the Ark of God with others sailing across the spiritual sea of time and the cosmos.

Even though all I hear at times is an injurious cacophony of my Protestant past because I was back-handed in the head with the Bible; He continues to fine tune my soul so I can hear the great symphony of the chorus of faith.

I still laugh with my wife when some phrase comes up in casual conversation and we both bust out singing Protestant hymns at the same time—*Amazing grace how sweet the sound.* Those hymns are never far from my whistling lips. I send my children to Catholic schools and am blessed by having holy Catholic friends who always included me in their lives of faith. I love the Episcopalians and how they accept everyone. I'm intrigued by fresh thinkers and writers of the 'Emergent church' movements. I know He works beyond my under-standings and interpretations of any divine revelations to work healing in not only my soul but in the other spiritually wounded as well.

We are not alone. He is not passive. I believe God, the Hound of heaven, is hunting everywhere. There is no place or time in history or present scenario where His love cannot reach and heal. I can't say where God does not work. I only know where He has worked in history and where He works now, specifically in Eastern Orthodoxy.

The Eastern Orthodox Church is not without its flaws. Major cultural hurdles must be addressed if anybody dares to venture to her. It is not an existentially easy journey to make. The inner spiritual work is painful because in her Tradition one is exposed to the bitter-sweet crucible of holiness and an all burning divine love. But if anybody walks into that Church building and looks up at the large icon in the apse of Mary with Christ sitting on His throne (her lap) and see a welcoming embrace to His life giving sacraments, then it's a banquet I believe the spiritually wounded will be thankful for attending. It's a worldview shattering experience to dance like this with the Triune God but what a dance it is.

God authentically, mysteriously, confusingly, but unmistakably works in the life of the Orthodox Church. The Spirit of Truth hovers over the Body of Christ as it lives within its mystical and sacramental traditions, weeping icons, angelic visits, saintly apparitions, miracle-working relics of saints. The Spirit of Truth works dynamically through the authority of the bishops, priests, monks, and nuns who rightly interpret and apply the Bible in perfect harmony with the apostolic understanding and in unity with what all Christians everywhere and at all times have believed. This truth guiding tradition is tangibly demonstrated throughout time in the love among the laity and in the making of saints. It is through Eastern Orthodoxy's synergy of the physical and spiritual realities that I am assured that I am loved by God. I am not alone. I am safe to heal from my spiritual injuries no matter how often I raise my fist to God or must unlearn versions of Him.

St. Paul, aside from Jesus, lived one of the most amazing life's in human history. He chose to be a celibate; that right there rockets him up the list. He was a young Pharisee superstar—an award winning 'preacher boy'. He orchestrated a Torah assassination and watched the first Christian martyr die—St. Stephen the deacon. He saw the risen Lord and it blinded him. He spent three years unlearning God. He had mystical experiences to the third heaven—wherever that is. He taught amazing truths. He penned most of the New Testament. He planted and grew Christianity all across the Roman Empire. He battled a 'thorn in his flesh' given to him by Satan himself. He lived on the run, homeless and worked making tents for a living. He survived a shipwreck only to be beheaded for his faith. He was a citizen of the Roman Empire and the kingdom of God at the same time. He lived an amazing life.

Having lived that amazing life; having journeyed everywhere terrestrially and celestially he writes about a 'more excellent way' in one of the most endeared passages in history:

> Though I speak with the tongues of men and of angels, but have not love, I have become sounding brass or a clanging cymbal. [2] And though I have the gift of prophecy, and understand all mysteries and all knowledge, and though I have all faith, so that I could remove mountains, but have not love, I am nothing. [3] And though I bestow all my goods to feed the poor, and though I give my body to be burned, but have not love, it profits me nothing.
>
> [4] Love suffers long and is kind; love does not envy; love does not parade itself, is not puffed up; [5] does not behave rudely, does not seek its own, is not

provoked, thinks no evil; [6] does not rejoice in iniquity, but rejoices in the truth; [7] bears all things, believes all things, hopes all things, endures all things. [8] Love never fails. But whether there are prophecies, they will fail; whether there are tongues, they will cease; whether there is knowledge, it will vanish away. [9] For we know in part and we prophesy in part. [10] But when that which is perfect has come, then that which is in part will be done away.

[11] When I was a child, I spoke as a child, I understood as a child, I thought as a child; but when I became a man, I put away childish things. [12] For now we see in a mirror, dimly, but then face to face. Now I know in part, but then I shall know just as I also am known.

[13] And now abide faith, hope, love, these three; but the greatest of these is love. [119]

In my journey, my less than *excellent* way, I have long laid down my 'rifle' and would not claim that God is not at work, hunting, healing and reconciling in other Christian traditions or even in some unfathomable, mysterious way all of humanity with her sacred expressions trying to connect with the Divine. My job is to love everyone who gets in my way and hope for the salvation and redemption of every creature— even the devil. Love your enemies, right?

It was not my intention in writing this memoir to dispar-

---

[119] I Corinthians 13: 1-13.

age anyone's 'journey' toward God nor was it to embarrass or embitter anyone referenced. I have journeyed down many roads: The Bible only-'fighting fundy' Baptist, the young hip Christian who was into the 'Emergent church' movement, the tired of believing 'all those hypocrites' agnostic, the total liberal conglomeration of spirituality, and even the lapsed Orthodox who thinks the Orthodox Church is a dead 'old country' religion. On those roads, those journeys, even when it felt like a dead end, God met me there.

I now believe we are all travelling and trying to find a life of love—that most excellent way. We are all participating in each other's cosmic, sacred and divine journeys. I now feel grateful appreciation for my fellow sojourners who travel this path towards the banquet of God, this 'most excellent way'.

> "God creates out of nothing. Wonderful you say.
> Yes, to be sure, but he does what is still more won-
> derful: he makes saints out of sinners."[120]

Through Eastern Orthodoxy, God has taken sinful, spiritually injured people, like me, and healed them by making love a reality for them and giving them the divine energy to put that love into action. Through her life giving waters of baptism, sacraments, and traditions He has remade sinners into saints: Photini,[121] the sexually scandalous woman at the

---

[120] Soren Kierkegaard: Journal entry: July 7, 1838

[121] Tradition teaches us that the Samaritan woman at the well (John 4:5-42) became a great evangelist and was re-named Photini- the enlightened one.

well who was so thirsty for love. Saul/St. Paul, the architect of a religious persecution, St. Moses the Ethiopian, a murder, St. Mary of Egypt, a harlot, St. Augustine, a sex crazed partier, on and on personal histories tell us about how the transformational love of God has healed and transformed lives.

I still struggle with doubts about sacred realities and find myself still unlearning God in my thoughts of faith, even in Eastern Orthodoxy. Many times it makes no sense whatsoever. It's foolish. It's hard to rationalize yet I find it true the more I practice it—a relational epistemology of spiritual truth. Orthodoxy is a spiritual reality beyond my reason. But I must continue to press on through all the suffering and angst of life to find my true self living in God's love, in God's community, in God's Church that 'the gates of hell will not prevail against'. [122]

So much good and so many little hells in everybody's existence—I don't know how to reconcile it all. How does suffering lead to good? God's answer to Job and all his sufferings was, 'hey, who do you think you are? And do you know who the hell I am?' [123] What kind of answer is that?

I am often left with unanswered questions about how it all

---

[122] "And I also say to you that you are Peter, and on this rock I will build My church, and the gates of Hades shall not prevail against it" (Matthew 16:18).

[123] "Who is this who darkens counsel by words without knowledge? Now prepare yourself like a man; I will question you, and you shall answer Me. 'Where were you when I laid the foundations of the earth? Tell Me, if you have understanding" (Job 38:2-4; Job chapters 38-41).

works together for good for those who love God.[124] And there are too many 'why' questions that are simply beyond me. I don't have all the answers; neither does anyone else though. We are all compelled towards the flickers of divinity we see in this life.

I journey limping along towards the kingdom of God trying to truly love others while practicing Eastern Orthodox Christianity over other Christian traditions and religions. I was lost and injured in the 'far country' of Protestantism. I became a spiritually prodigal son who needed to come to his senses, make his way back and be embraced and healed by a loving Father God who runs down my wayward path to find me, collect me in his arms and celebrate my return.[125]

It's a hard journey for sure but I don't lose hope. I don't because there is love in the world; and that is the greatest way of all three that St. Paul tells us about—the saint making way.

I have one last outstanding wager with God. My end of the bargain is to continue to search for this transformational and healing love that makes saints of sinners. It is hidden and often elusive due to cultural disconnects and my misunderstandings of the Eastern Orthodox Church in America. But I cannot give up.

His end is that His dynamic, mystical, sacramental and relational love that has changed sinners into saints in the past will work for me, R. Leo Olson, a former biblical assassin,

---

[124] "And we know that all things work together for good to those who love God, to those who are the called according to His purpose" (Romans 8:28).

[125] Parable of the prodigal son (Luke 15:11-31).

still healing from spiritual head injuries.

In this last divine wager I really need the 'House to win'.